Copyright © 2018 Léa Mai Nguyen
All rights reserved.
ISBN: 978-1-7326444-0-3

OF MICE AND MUSES

The Creative Journey Behind

La Crème de la Crème

of Mouse taxidermy

by
Léa Mai Nguyen
with
Patricia Fitzsimmons

Table of Contents

DEDICATION 6

ACKNOWLEDGMENTS 7

BUT FIRST, LET'S TALK ABOUT ME 9

In the Beginning Were Computers 11

Fanfiction 14

Live from the Leathery 17

Mouses 26

Headmounts 41

Selling a Product 45

A DAY IN THE LIFE I 58

TRIUMPHS AND DISASTERS 64

Attack of the Killer Moths 65

Conventions, Balls, and other such Events 67

Jenny Lawson a.k.a. The Bloggess 72

The Pet Snacks 74

The Studio Visits 75

The Buzzfeed Article 76

Henri Souris 79

The Art Deco Lamp 84

Geoff Vassallo 85

The Rehydrating Mice 86

A DAY IN THE LIFE II 90
LA CRÈME DE LA CRÈME 97

Safari Hunters 99
Gnomes 104
Grim Reapers 109
Little Red Riding Hood 114
Mad Hatter 120
Supreme Court Justice Ruth Bader Ginsburg 124
Mouseguard 126
The Log Lady 128
Harry Potter 130
Carmen Miranda 132
Miss Havisham 135

A DAY IN THE LIFE III 139
AT LAST, TAXIDERMY INSTRUCTIONS 144

Procuring the mouse 145
Supplies 146
Skinning 153
Stuffing 162
Posing 175
Outfits 176

CONCLUSION 177

About the Authors 180

DEDICATION

I dedicate this book to my wife Diane and to my son Victor: thank you for allowing me to explore new and exciting things, and for supporting my weird creative endeavors.

To Patricia, my Muse, who came on this adventure with me, not knowing it would involve dead animals, steampunk conventions, countless hours of research, and putting up with my general ignorance about literary and historical matters.

ACKNOWLEDGMENTS

The biggest thanks to my father-in-law, Charlie Caliva, who changed my life by passing on his leather tools to me.

My mom and my sister, who are always supportive of anything I come up with.

My dad, who taught me not to listen to bullies, especially him.

I want to thank Paxton Gate, Geoff Vassallo and Michael Levy for helping me discover the world of taxidermy and giving me the desire and the opportunity to sell my own work.

Thank you to Barbara Andino-Stevenson, my clay teacher, for encouraging me on the path to self-employment.

Thank you to Joel Aron, who showed me how to take good photographs and who so generously gave me the camera I've been using for three years now.

Lori Muttersbach, the best unexpected copy editor I could ever wish for. Thank you for your dedicated and relentless efforts in expunging all the mistakes from this book.

Tonja, Sheila, and all the picnic girls who would dutifully Ooh and Aaah through all the stages of my quest to find my own thing.

Chris and Kevin, my friends and GURPS (Generic Universal Role Playing System) playing buddies of 20 years and still counting.

My thanks to Sophie, my old friend from art school, for never changing and for always being excited at discovering new things.

Kim, my ex-work wife, Jed and Stacey, and Rhoda, my friends from Telltale, thank you for putting up with my sporadic friendship. Thank you to Stacey's mom, for always looking out for stuff that I might be able to use for the mice.

Napoleon Bonaparte.
Contrary to popular belief, Napoleon wasn't short. He simply would pick very tall bodyguards to surround him.

But first, let's talk about me

Hello, my name is Mai, I am a Mouse Taxidermist.

Had you told me, even a few years ago, that I would say that one day, I would have laughed in disbelief at the very idea. Laughed and laughed and laughed!

I am about to embark on a very self-indulgent tale about how I stumbled upon the art of taxidermy. If you are mainly interested in the process, go right ahead and skip to the last chapter: "At last, taxidermy instructions".

The origins of taxidermy are lost in the mists of history; indeed, preserved animals were found in the excavated tombs of several Egyptian Pharaohs. The boy king Tutankhamun himself was laid to rest in the Valley of the Kings with various taxidermied animals to keep him company in the afterlife.

But the "Golden Age" of taxidermy came about in the Victorian era. At the Great Exhibition of 1851 held at the Crystal Palace in London's Hyde Park, an English ornithologist called John Hancock installed an exhibit of mounted birds which proved to be immensely popular with the crowds. After this came a great surge of interest in the art of preserving and mounting animals in a lifelike manner. Collections proliferated and preserved birds became almost de rigueur in every middle- and upper-class Victorian home. Indeed, Queen Victoria herself amassed a fine collection.

Taxidermists were also increasingly employed by bereaved pet owners to stuff their dear departed dogs and cats, thus conferring upon the animals a kind of immortality.

Later in the 19th century a style known as "anthropomorphic taxidermy" became very popular. For this, mounted animals (kittens and baby rabbits) were dressed in miniature human clothes and posed as if engaged in human activities. Also increasingly popular were bizarrely malformed animals such as four-legged chickens and two-headed lambs. The majority of them had not been malformed in life, but artists eager to exploit the public's unceasing demand for sensation and freakish thrills had frankensteined them together post-mortem.

Nowadays of course, taxidermy might best be described as a service industry for hunters.

The vast majority of animal mounts are produced as hunting trophies or for museum displays. They are mounted realistically, prowling, jumping; posed as if still alive in their natural habitat.

Then there's a small subset that does taxidermy as oddities, for display in curio cabinets.

The only reason I do taxidermy is that it provides me with figures for which I can design and create costumes and accessories.

And it was all an accident...

Note that I will use the words "mice", "meeces" and "mouses" as if they were all correct. Because the English language doesn't make any sense anyway. I should know, I'm French.

In the Beginning Were Computers

I had been working in computer/video games since 1994. I started just after attending the Ecole Nationale des Arts Décoratifs in Paris. My Ultimate Goal was to be a TV director and/or writer, after ditching my childhood Ultimate Goal of being a graphic novel artist.

My career in games happened by chance, right after art school, but I fully embraced it. It was both artistic and technical, and I immediately fell in love. I was good at it too.

The following year, I applied at LucasArts, George Lucas' game division, and was hired. I moved to the US, and a few years later in 2000 I met my wife Diane through work. She worked next door at Industrial Light and Magic (ILM). In 2003 we had a son, Victor.

After 10 years at LucasArts, I left to join Telltale, which was started by ex-LucasArts employees to carry on the adventure game genre. I stayed with Telltale for 7 years and saw them grow from fifteen to over a hundred employees.

In 2012 I started as the art director for a small game studio located in downtown San Francisco and whose three founders were also ex-Lucas. My world is a small world.

Every morning I would take the ferry, often through the fog, from Marin County to downtown San Francisco, and very much enjoyed my healthy 25 minute walks to and from the office. I liked my bosses and co-workers, I liked my job. All was well.

In the summer of 2012, my father-in-law had given me a heavy trunk full of all his leather-working tools. His deteriorating sight and shaky hands would no longer allow him to practice his hobby, and he had accumulated a goodly amount of material and tools.

As the artist in the family, it made sense that I would be interested in the trunk and its contents.

However, when you're presented with a huge selection of curiously shaped, shiny metal bits that you'd never seen or used before, it's somewhat overwhelming. I didn't even know where to start.

I'm ashamed to admit that we stored the trunk in the garage and forgot all about it.

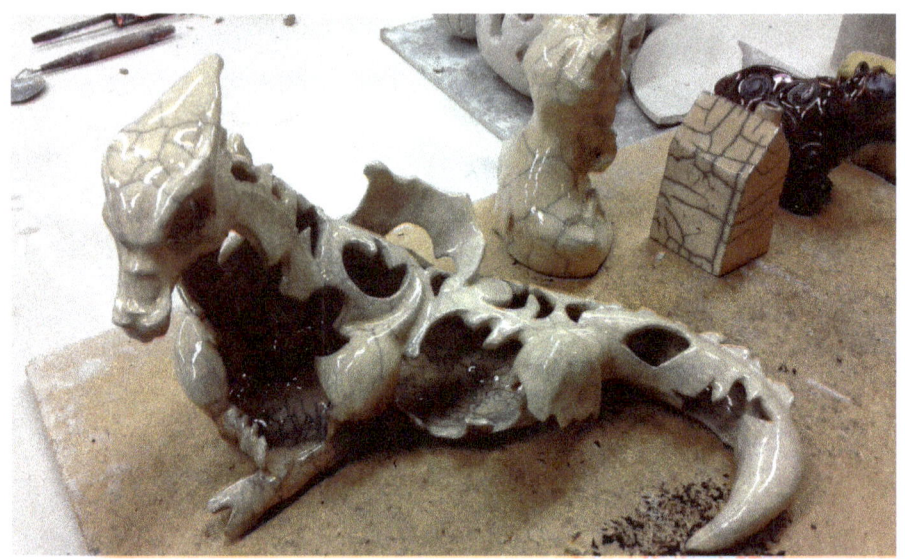

Clay Dragon Bones

When my son was younger, I attended a clay class with him for a few years.
Barbara, the teacher, was wonderful. She would always help you achieve a desired result with a particular technique, and when you lost control of your vase on the wheel, Barbara would take over the droopy mess and make it stand again in half a second with her magic fingers.
If you lost your inspiration, she would ask you questions until you found your own answer and were able to move on.
No matter the issue, she would just gently guide you back on track, not unlike the way a kung-fu master is able to deflect energy and redirect it towards his opponent. In this case a friend, not foe.
Every piece was entirely your own, yet you learned new tricks every time.
Barbara is a true, wise master.
If I were a teacher, I would like to be like Barbara. It will never happen because I have no patience with people.

Besides fan fiction, I've always had creative side projects: fairy trap, gris-gris, magic wand.

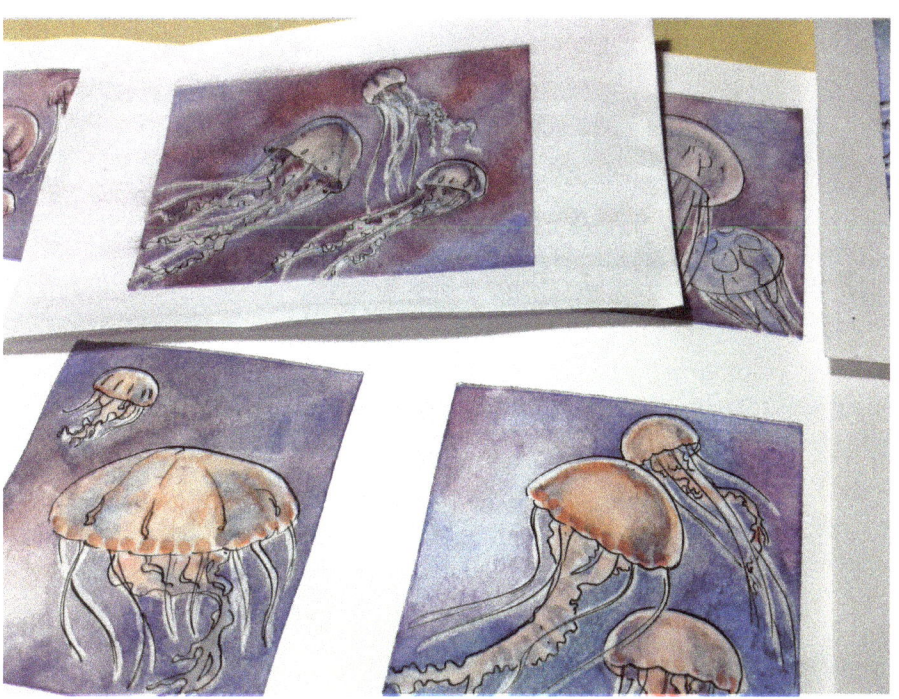

Jellyfish watercolors.

Fanfiction

I have always had a lot of creative side projects, and one of them was writing lesbian fan fiction. Is there any other kind of fan fiction? I think not.

I would write almost every day, from after dinner to about 11:00 at night. I could write 1500-2500 words in a couple of hours and I would post each chapter on the website as I went.

If you're a writer, it's a very good exercise in discipline, to have to post every day and continue where you left off. You have to deal with what you wrote before without being able to go back and edit it. And you get people writing to you and encouraging you along the way. I found it very rewarding.

Anyway, at the time, my big endeavor as an amateur writer was an epic Jack the Ripper AU (alternate universe for the newbies). I had no idea it would involve so much research. Before that, I had exclusively written "first time" stories that involved two women stumbling from the couch to the bedroom in a flurry of discarded garments. Hmmm…

Writing the first chapter of the Jack the Ripper story was incredibly slow and painful. I had to turn to the internet for every sentence I would write.

For example, how would a single woman travel from New York to London in the year 1888? What professions, if any, would be open to women back then? How would an unmarried, English noblewoman of 30 years of age be regarded? Did she have access to her own money, or would she still be dependent on her parents' wealth?

Having been born and raised in France by a German mother and a Vietnamese father, English history and manners is not something that came easily to me.

Initially expecting to conclude the story in about 6 chapters, which was my usual fare, I was still laboring with the beginnings of the investigation by chapter 9, which is when a reader from Dorset, England contacted me. She had written to say how much she enjoyed my stories, and she must have sensed my struggle, because she very politely offered her help in 'Anglicizing' some of my prose. She was a born and bred Londoner, and well-read in everything Ripper, not least because she had gone to school in the East End of London, the area where Jack committed his terrible crimes. I can see now that she must have recoiled in horror at my inept attempt at Victorian writing.

You're probably wondering where I'm going with this. Be patient. If I hadn't encountered Patricia, there would be no mice.

As I said, Patricia was her name, a retired civil servant, and by chapter 11, we were a team. She would correct my Americanisms and became my historical adviser. We would discuss plot points before I would write anything. I would send her every chapter to proof read and edit before publishing it.

Patricia provided me with a magic mirror, indirectly questioning if I was doing my best; if I could do even better. By offering advice and asking questions, she would make me think deeper, and often I would end up dismissing my flawed, initial ideas to find fresh ones along a path I wouldn't have found by myself.

I wanted to be a better writer for her, and it worked.

I had found my Muse.

The following summer, my father-in-law asked me:

"Mai, have you looked at the leather tools yet?"

I was embarrassed: "No."

He told me: "Bring back the trunk, I'll show you how to use them."

So he did. I watched eagerly as he demonstrated the basics of leather work, and explained every single tool in the trunk.

Now I could start at the beginning and I couldn't wait to take it back home and get to work!

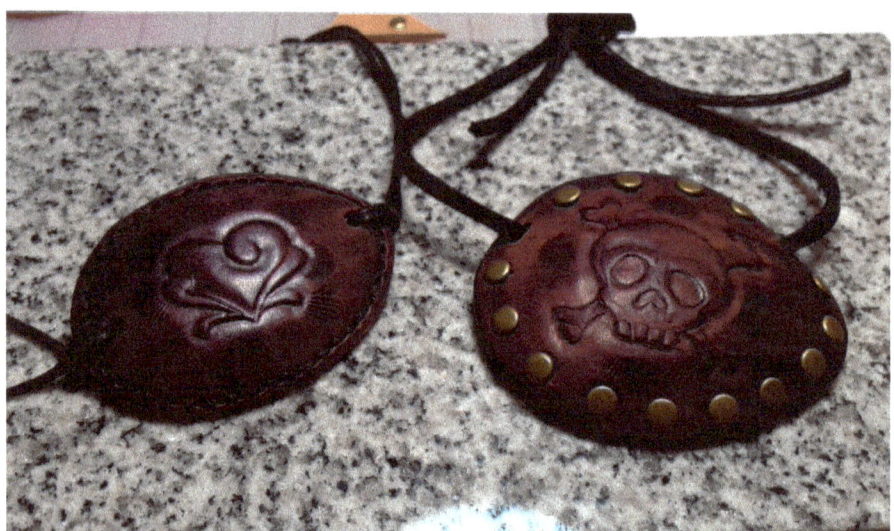

After Grandpa showed me the leather tools, I was able to get to work on all sorts of leather projects, like eyepatches.

Live from the Leathery

When I started doing leatherwork, the fanfiction slowed down, but Patricia was still helping me along. I was making bracelets, belts and obvious leather accessories, like pirate eyepatches. YouTube provided a lot of resources on how to do things, and I could turn to eBay for supplies that I couldn't find at my craft store.

More than any of my other hobbies, which included drawing, painting, sewing, and lots more, I loved leather craft because I was working with my hands, and I could do everything in my own office, at home. I could touch and feel what I was making, it was here to stay.

I had enthusiastically worked on computers for 20 years, and had nothing tangible to show for it. Digital formats come and go, especially in games.

That's when I finally realized that, even though I liked my job, there was nothing for me beyond the horizon any more.

I was ready for a break.

It was also a time where I realized life is too short just to sit and watch it pass by in front of a screen. I used to love movies and watching TV, but in my early thirties, it made me squirm to sit and do nothing. Watching something was too passive.

I turned to playing games, where at least I could tell myself I was doing something, even while sitting on the couch. But in the end, I was still consuming somebody else's work and not producing anything of my own.

When I turned forty, even games turned stale. It was just as unproductive as watching TV. I couldn't stand it. I had to be doing or making something.

And now not even working at a games studio seemed satisfying enough.

I discussed it with Diane, and I asked if I could take a sabbatical. After crunching some numbers, we figured we could last four months on one salary. Then I'd go back to work, or find some freelance contracts.

I quit my job and went to work for myself.

I would still get up with the rest of the family, make lunches for everybody, kiss them goodbye and send them off to school and work.

Patricia had been watching the BBC's production of "Bleak House" by Charles Dickens. One of the characters, Mr John Jarndyce, had a special room in his house into which he would retreat to growl when he was out of humour with the world. Mr Jarndyce named his special room the Growlery.

When I reorganized my office to be more suited for leatherwork, Patricia started calling my office the Leathery, after the Growlery. The name stuck.

At 8:00 AM, I'd be in the Leathery, and would call Patricia on Skype. In England, it was 4PM.

We would spend all morning together, discussing new ideas. She would research while I worked, and she would give me feedback on everything during the whole process. When I worked for long stretches at a time, we would choose a book and she would read to us. She's a very good reader.

We would split for lunch, her dinner, since she's 8 hours ahead, and we would resume for the afternoon/evening.

She would sign off as my son would come home from school in the afternoon. Around 6:00 PM I would stop working and make dinner for the family. I'd often go back to the Leathery after dinner, because Diane likes to relax with some TV after work.

The perfect life.

Transforming the office into a Leathery.

There can be no leatherwork without a granite slab to work on.

I came up with the name "Le Heart", because I'm French. I'm neither here nor there about it, but I really liked the stylized heart logo that I made.

It's curious how, when you start something, you feel compelled to find a company name and make yourself a logo right away. When I see other people do it, I roll my eyes at them. I think "Figure out what you're going to do first. Start something and finish it, then you can come up with a logo. The logo is not the priority. Your product is!"

But somehow if you don't start with a logo, you don't feel like you're starting at all. You need to set your logo first, just as troops listen to the bugle call to set off. No logo, no start.

The first Le Heart logo.

I began with bracelets, and tooled belt buckles.

Patricia would send me ancient buckles and decorative pieces of harness from Roman and Saxon times to Victorian which she had purchased from eBay. These artifacts had been unearthed by England's army of metal detectorists. I used them and integrated them into my crafts.

After two months, I thought "Where am I going with this?"

The thing is, Diane, who is very wise and wonderful, had agreed to let me stop work for about four months. That's all we could afford. Cutting our income in half was a very big deal. We have a mortgage and a kid, and bills to pay.

Yet I was secretly hoping I wouldn't have to go back to work, if only I could figure out how to make money with my leatherwork.

There was no way I could make money with my leatherwork. Browsing eBay and other stores, I very quickly realized I couldn't compete with the craftsmanship and prices that were out there, mostly from China. I was soon three months into my sabbatical, and still had not stumbled upon an obvious product that I felt could earn me a living.

Luckily, there's one thing that happens when you do something that makes you happy, beyond the weekly paycheck: you stop spending money on frivolous, useless things. Where previously you would go shopping to reward yourself for a hard week's work, the work itself is your reward. Cutting expenses on my side just happened and didn't require any effort at all. I even enjoyed waiting weeks or months to buy a tool, or a piece of fabric, until I had no other choice. I would tell myself: "I need to sell four headmounts for this". And I'd wait until I reached the goal. Working with my hands was my joy. I didn't need any extras. The hard part was refraining from scolding Diane for spending the money she worked hard to earn just so I could stay off the street corner.

Octopus belt buckle.

Fleur de lys belt buckle.

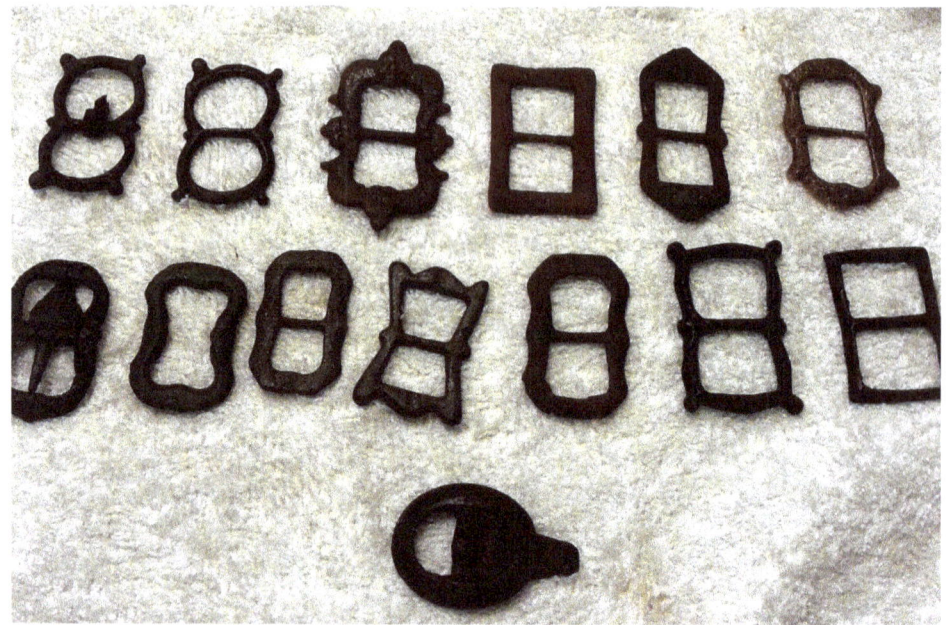

Antique buckles from Patricia.

Bracelets with antique buckles and Celt ring money.

Leather Scarab

One day I fashioned a large scarab beetle using tooling leather which I soaked in hot water. I pinned the leather over a sculpted form whilst it was wet and as it dried, it retained its shape. The scarab gave me a glorious idea. I could shape leather! I could make leather armor! Those clever Romans used to employ a similar technique to produce some of their armor. The technique is called "cuir bouilli", which in French literally means "boiled leather". To this day, I still love trying to teach Patricia how to say "cuir bouilli" with the correct French pronunciation. Of course she declares that these two words are impossible for a non-Frenchie to get their tongue around, but oh my goodness it is fun watching her try!

You try it. Cuir bouilli. Cuir. Bouilli. Queer. Boo-Yee.

Never mind, where was I? Oh yes,

I could make a tiny, miniature suit of armor for an action figure!

No. I didn't want a plastic figure if I was to use real leather. Something natural, about the size of… a mouse.

Mouses

Admittedly, I had taken a taxidermy class a few years back.

Diane had seen an online post for taxidermy classes at Paxton Gate, a taxidermy store in San Francisco. She knows I'm not one to take classes. I get bored too easily.

So as any good wife would do, she asked if she could show me what she wanted to get me for Christmas, and if it would be something I'd like.

She hid the computer screen, I walked over, and upon the dramatic reveal, I said "Yes!"

The class was taught by a wonderful teacher called Geoff Vassallo.

Geoff is a real, traditional taxidermist. He is a hunter and works with hunters. He does big game such as deer, bears and alligators. When he was younger, he apprenticed with traditional taxidermists and those are the techniques he uses.

He now owns Wilderness taxidermy in Fremont, California. Paxton Gate hosts his classes regularly, and they include rooster, squirrel, mouse, jackelopes, and rabbit mounts.

In that one-day class, I made an ugly Guinea Fowl, because everybody else grabbed the pretty roosters with the colorful plumage.

Even though I have never made another bird since, it was enough to take the mystery out of the process. And now, years later, I could apply what I remembered from the Paxton Gate class to a tiny rodent.

The angry Guinea Fowl I mounted in my first taxidermy class.

Taxidermy is not an exact craft. Every taxidermist has their own way of doing things, and always looks for new techniques to get faster and better results. There is no right or wrong, just what works for you and what you want to achieve.

As always, I turned to YouTube to watch how to taxidermy a mouse as opposed to a bird.

Back then, all the way back in 2014, mouse taxidermy artists would use a ball of twine or yarn to stuff the mouse, and they didn't use armature in the limbs. It's actually still the case for most of them. To me, the results often looked like a blob. Cute, but still a blob, and the mouse's features weren't defined enough for what I wanted to do.

I went to the pet shop and got a frozen feeder mouse to be my armor-clad soldier.

Because I wanted an anthropomorphic pose, I used white craft foam (from the floral arrangement section of the craft store) and carved a body that was the correct size and shape. I sculpted the head out of polymer clay so I could get as close as possible to a real mouse head.

Once the mouse was done and drying, it took me a few days to shape the leather and sew the armor together. I made a metal helmet out of a soda can. I had to buy a tool called a doming block for the purpose. It's a beautiful object, very tactile. It's made entirely out of metal and very heavy. Patricia immediately fell in love with it and coveted it. She still claims she'll buy one, even though she has absolutely no use for it.

Shaping leather armor.

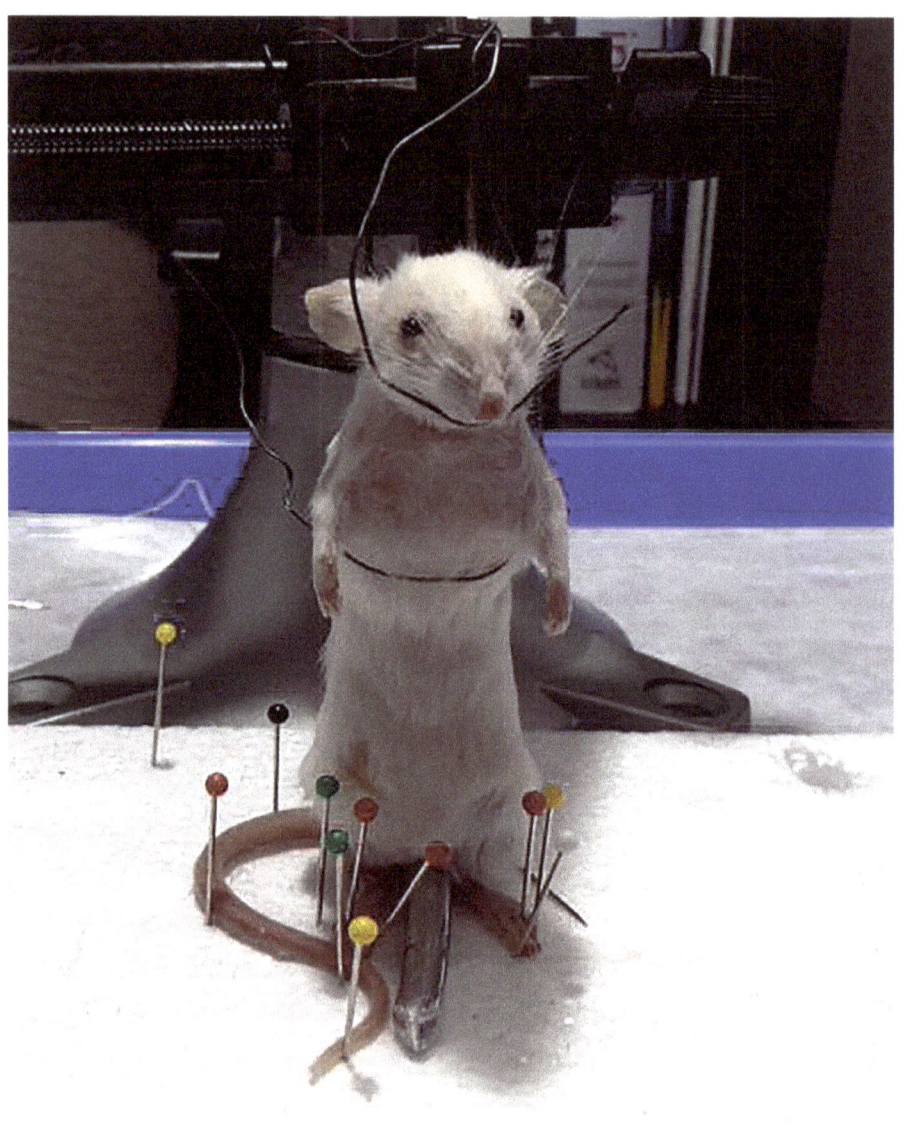

Look, it's a mouse torture device!
It makes me cringe now, but this is what happens when you don't use armature in the limbs. I guess I hadn't put any wires for the neck either, or only a flimsy one.
In order to get a pose that allowed him to stand, I cobbled an emergency gibbet to hold the mouse up while drying.

My first finished mouse

After that I sewed the outfit on top of the mouse, working around the now rigid head and limbs.

This was before I figured out that the best method is to make the costume first and the mouse last.

I know it's ugly. There's no armature in the limbs, it's standing on its heels, and the spine is still inside the tail. The face is elongated and the eyes are too small.

But it was my first, I finished it, and I was very proud of it.

I was going to make a whole chess set out of Roman soldiers! All 32 pieces!

32 PIECES?

I don't think so.

That's when I came across an eBay listing for some really, really thin, bone-white leather. When it arrived, I could see that the leather was so fine, I could use it to sew actual tiny clothes. I had a good selection of leather dyes now and I could use them to dye the outfits any color I wanted.

I could make a pattern to fit a mouse, and sew an actual coat. So I did.

Patricia researched the styles and accessories, and I made a sleeveless coat for my first Steampunk mouse. I didn't know much about Steampunk back then, but I would now describe it as Victorian Science Fiction. Think Jules Verne and H.G. Wells, Captain Nemo, The Nautilus and The Time Machine. Besides the coat, accessories included a leather top hat, a shoulder bag, a belt, a cravat, some tiny nailheads for buttons, and I even devised a method for making miniature goggles using leather lacing, clear epoxy, and metal jump rings.

This time I put armature in the limbs, and used bigger beads for the eyes. The result isn't dramatically improved, but I was learning fast. He's still standing on his haunches, but he was to be the last one to do so.

My second mouse.

Though Patricia was initially horrified by the idea of taxidermy, she could see that I respected the mice, which I do, and she did enjoy doing the research. And she was the perfect researcher! She knew the names of garments and accessories that I would describe, knew the style and period I could only guess at, and she's a fount of knowledge for just about anything you can think of. And you would think everybody knows how to use Google, but she would come up with results that wouldn't show up for me!

Patricia and I discussed, at length and in great detail, how we would design, classify and organize characters. We decided that I would make five of each design, and each character would have a name. The last name, or family name would be the same for all the characters in the series, but the first name would be different and would make them individuals.

Patricia would confuse me by referring to Christian names and surnames (the way they do in England). Upon seeing my confusion she rolled her eyes and sighed pityingly and said, just for me, we would call them first names and last names. Much better!

She would come up with the lists of potential names, and that was good enough for me. English is not my mother tongue and I don't have a sense for Anglo-Saxon names.

The first series was called Judd. A good old English name, so I'm told. The mice were roughly the same design as the prototype, but this time they stood on their toes. The faces looked considerably better, and the pose was much improved. Still a little stiff, but I was getting there.

I wanted them to look like a good quality finished product that I could sell. I looked around for potential pedestals, but I needed them to be hollow inside so I could mount the mice and tuck in the wires underneath, where they would be safely out of sight. It quickly became apparent that I would have to construct the pedestals myself.

I bought a compound saw and a quantity of ornate frame mouldings, and I made my own boxes on which to place the mice. I thought they looked great, and that's how I mounted all my early mice.

Abigail Judd.

Nusskracker.

Grace Savage, the vampire hunter.

Making frame moulding pedestals.

Brocklebank patterns.

Brocklebanks coats.

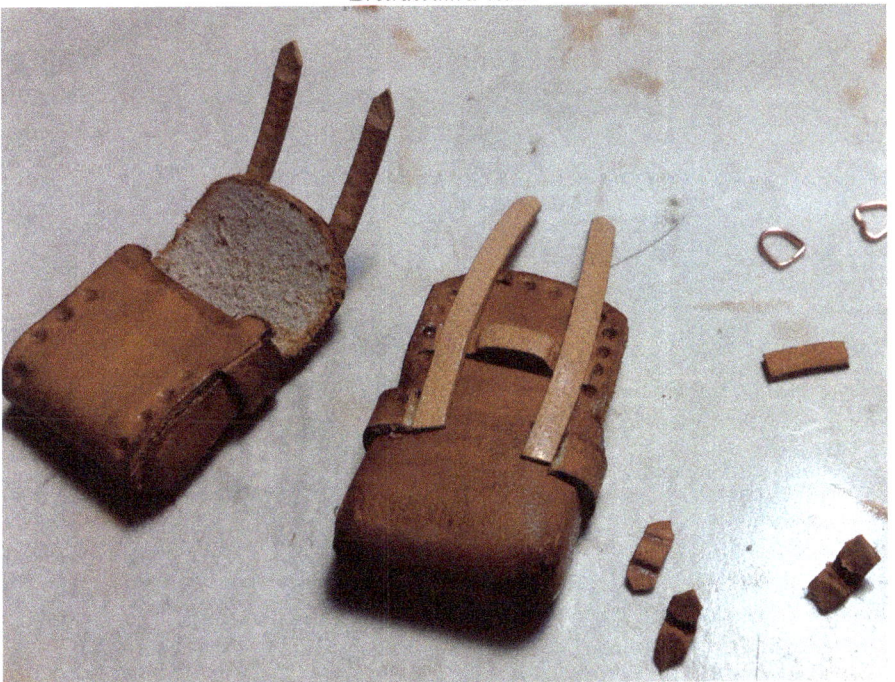
Brocklebanks bags.

Of course each mouse I made showed improvements; both aesthetically and technically. I made a little silicone mold for pressing the polymer clay head, so the sculpting would go faster. After completing a few designs, I could adapt new patterns by altering the shapes and length of coats and other clothes, so I wouldn't always have to start from scratch.

Most mice now took on average about four days to make, if nothing went wrong. And plenty could go wrong.

The fun part with each new design was the constant challenge of having to hand craft each item. I wasn't about to buy dollhouse accessories. I really wanted to make everything from scratch. I had to learn how to make paper patterns for the garments and how to work with wood, metal and leather. When I had done all that, I then had to master the art of adapting every technique to a miniature scale.

I became very good at scrounging for little bits and pieces that are part of every day life, such as hair pins, jewelry findings and electronics. I would take them apart or reassemble them in different ways to make what I wanted.

When I had my five Judds, I took one to the Paxton Gate store in San Francisco, where I had taken my first class six years earlier, and the buyer seemed impressed with my work. They took it on consignment, and that was the beginning of my Mouse taxidermy career.

I consequently made several designs, but because it took so long to make the outfits and accessories, it meant my prices were high. Even at $500 retail price, I was paid less than minimum wage for my efforts.

Due to the very nature of the product, namely mixing taxidermy with custom outfits, they couldn't possibly be mass-produced at a lower cost.

Another option was to move from the craft market to art, and have gallery shows instead, but having gone to art school, I know that in order to do art, you are expected to provide a message, something beyond an anecdotal, physical representation. I had always rolled my eyes at the very idea, even when I had to present my assignments to the class and the teachers. I had done it, and it just wasn't me. I would never be able to lie and invent a persona and message that felt contrived and artificial. I was inventing characters and telling a little story, no more, no less.

I simply needed a more affordable product.

Headmounts

This time it was my wife who came up with the idea. She had gone shopping at a novelty clothing store and among the knickknacks displayed by the register, she spotted a plastic miniature headmount of a stag.

She came home and shared her discovery. After a good ponder about how to make them, I started making real mouse headmounts.

Again, the first ones were rather ugly, but Paxton Gate seemed enchanted with them and took them in as well. They didn't have anything like it.

Despite the exquisite charm of the full mouses, their cost does make them a considered purchase, but if after consideration it turns out one couldn't afford it, as often happened, one could always buy a headmount, see?

So while the full mice drew all the attention, the headmounts would become my bread and butter.

Sculpting heads took hours...

Sculpting little polymer clay heads by hand was very tedious and time consuming. Eventually I made little silicone molds and I now pour them out of epoxy resin.

Unfortunately, the headmounts produced a huge surplus of skinless mice that I was loath to throw away. My cat really liked them but could only eat so many.

When our son was little we used to take him to the Wildcare Center in San Rafael to watch them feed the animals. They do a wonderful job, rescuing injured animals and rehabilitating them wherever possible, or keeping them safe at the Center if they cannot be released back into the wild. I hoped they might use my mice as food.

I called the Wildcare Center and left a message offering them a regular supply of frozen, skinned mice. That same day, a woman from the Center rang me back, somewhat confused. Had she heard right? Why did I have all these mice?

I explained the situation again, but she was more than a little concerned that I was catching wild mice, and said that the Center couldn't take them. I explained that no, I did not procure my mice by stalking them through the undergrowth armed with mousetraps, but that I ordered them frozen from Layne Labs, who raised clean and fresh feeder mice, and who claimed to kill them humanely.

It turned out that they order theirs from the same place, by the thousands, and yes, they would be happy to take my mice as well.

Since then, after I take the skin off the mice, I promptly return them to the freezer and every couple of months when I have enough I drop them off at the Wildcare Center. Doing this makes me feel a lot better about the taxidermy because no single part of the animal is wasted or thrown away. They were destined to be food for bigger creatures, and that's what they ultimately remain.

My first headmounts

Selling a Product

Early on I opened an Etsy shop and a seller account on Ebay. This is what I learned from the experience:

For both sites, I initially took pictures of each headmount and created a unique listing for every one. It was a lot of work and managing my inventory was tedious. Because people could favorite an item, as soon as the item sold, I would lose the "Favorite" score by having to make a new listing.

Ebay didn't sell well for me at all. Because the site is so huge with so many things for sale, my little mice got lost amidst the vast array of other items. I stopped using Ebay.

Whereas people who shop on Etsy are specifically looking for something handmade, original and unique. Look no further. C'est moi, as we say in France...

Over time, I learned to streamline my headmounts so I made just three or four different kinds. In the beginning, I had produced variations in the color of the mouse, several different colors of leather, and a selection of shapes, materials and colors for the frame itself. I wanted to offer variety. But what I actually did was to produce a nightmare of production management for myself. Making unique combinations, taking pictures of each one and creating individual listings was time consuming in the extreme. Also, it is just as confusing for the customer when you overwhelm them with too many choices.

So, away with the variety: I picked three kinds of frame I liked, did either a turquoise or red leather background, and did half dark, half white mice. I did all the same wooden shields, and all the same wooden antlers.

Now I could simply take a good set of pictures for each kind, leave the same listings up and just renew the quantity when I needed to. It also made it easier to know what sold well and when it was time to make more.

Because the listings accumulated Favorite scores and sold often enough, the headmounts would consistently stay in the first page of search results within Etsy, just below the advertised items.

This was my optimized lineup of headmounts on Etsy:

Eventually, even though I had been thinking about it for a while, I figured out how to make little antlers that I could secure onto the mouse heads. They are solid enough that they won't easily snap off. I made them short and stubby, so they wouldn't stick out beyond the borders of the escutcheon. I called them mouselopes, as opposed to the famous jackelopes, which feature a jackrabbit with antlers. The mouselopes ended up replacing the wooden antler escutcheons in my lineup.

After a year, it was clear that I was sticking to taxidermy and not going back. I thought we should have a tag line for my brand and when I mentioned this to Patricia she went quiet for a few minutes and then came up with "La Crème de la Crème of Mouse Taxidermy". I squealed, because it was absolutely perfect! It keeps the French theme, and says I'm the best without sounding too arrogant. Which I am. The best. And arrogant. Isn't every artist?

I also wanted to update my logo, and that's where, after a few seconds of doodling, the heart acquired little eyes and whiskers and morphed into a mouse head as if it had been planned all along!

Le Heart logo becomes a mouse.

At some point, someone suggested I should upgrade in size. I took a squirrel class with Geoff again, but it only confirmed that I was most comfortable working with mice. I wouldn't have been able to match the amount of detail I could cram onto a mouse to a squirrel. But I did finally learn how to deglove the tail!

In the class, both times attended by a majority of women, someone mentioned the Edwardian Ball, a two-day annual event held in San Francisco at the end of January. I had never heard of it. They featured an Artist Bazaar in the basement, and she thought I would fit right in.

I applied to be a vendor at the Bazaar, and was accepted.

What a fantastic experience! And although I did not, that first time, have a suitable outfit to wear, just the joy of being able to be face-to-face with my customers recharged my creative batteries for months. Seeing people giggle and squeal with delight at my mice was absolutely priceless. I did really well and ended up applying to a few other events every year after that. The Steampunk ones were the best, and I stuck to those, as well as the Nightlife Craft event at the California Academy of Sciences.

Alexander Dracul
This was the first time I made an open-mouthed mouse. I had to sculpt the head with an open mouth, tongue and fangs, paint it, then fit the skin over it and hope it would sit right. It took a couple of attempts before I achieved the correct shape and size.

Now you're doubtless thinking that everything was hunky-dory and that I have been able to make a very comfortable living from my mice. Alas not so. I could pay for my supplies, and sometimes I had a little extra to pay one month's mortgage, but overall I couldn't, and still can't, make a living out of taxidermy mice.

In the end Diane let me have my cake and eat it too. I've been free for three amazing years now. We did manage to cut expenses to the point where things are only really tight when it's time to pay our property taxes, and for this, I occasionally take freelance work in Games. A few weeks of freelancing pays more than all the mice I can sell in an entire year.

The moral of the story is that, even though I've always really enjoyed the jobs I've had, I've never been happier than I am now, making things with my hands.

I no longer live from weekend to weekend. I actually look forward to Monday mornings.

Nobody gets to tell me to put down my pencil because the deadline is up.

I'm able to finish things, and I'm the one who says when something is finished to my own standards. Your standards get higher as you learn and grow, and it's so rewarding to see your own progress over the months.

Art, or crafts, is all about practice. Whatever it is that you're interested in, nothing will get you there faster than just doing it.

You can read all the books in the world, watch hundreds of videos on YouTube, take class after class and ask your mentors, but nothing, nothing will replace just doing it. Even when your first time is a disaster, even if it's still not great by the fifth time.

And most importantly, finish what you've started. Every time. Even when it looks like crap in the middle, and crap in the end. You will discover and learn things at every stage, things that wouldn't occur to you had you not finished it. Finishing will inform the following start, and the next project will be better for it.

"We learn from failure, not from success!"

- Bram Stoker, Dracula.

Captain Bering. The Bering Sea and Bering Strait are named after this Danish explorer.

Captain Edward Smith was in charge of the Titanic on its maiden voyage.

Clint Shaw

Pete Shaw.
The cowboys were initially a commission. Note that all belts are properly buckled, and the handguns would fit in their holster were they not glued in the mouse's hand.

A Day in the Life I

MAI: Hello! Did you have dinner?

PATRICIA: Yes I did. I phoned for a fish and chips takeaway. I always order a small portion of chips and they keep sending me a mini Mount Everest of the bloody things... enough to feed at least seventeen people! And I only ate half of the haddock. I shall have the rest tomorrow. What did you have for your lunch?

MAI: Oh I made liver with onions and bacon. With a mashed potato pancake from yesterday's leftovers...

PATRICIA: Ah, my mum used to make great liver and onions. Scrummy! Right, so I posted some more stuff about old chemist storefronts on the Pinterest board for you, for the dentist diorama commission.

MAI: Yes I saw! Thank you! I really like the dentist chairs. No wonder dentists have such a horrible reputation. They were like torture chairs!

PATRICIA: You'll need to make small dentist tools. And vials.

MAI: I don't want to start on it too soon, before the guy commits to the custom mouse.

PATRICIA: Ah yes, that's prudent.

MAI: I think that regardless, I like the idea of a Victorian dentist, or those oil... snake... doctors? What is it?

PATRICIA: Oh you daft little French person... it's snake oil salesman. Or quack doctors.

MAI: I think I like quack doctors better.

PATRICIA: Will you do a wagon with vials and potions on display?

MAI: Mmmmhh... No, I think more like a regular mouse. It would take me too long if I do the whole scene, and I would have to price it too high.

PATRICIA: Fair enough, so a solo standing quack doctor. Male or female?

MAI: Oh yes, it's time for a woman.

PATRICIA: Lab coat over a dress? And a stethoscope, and one of those headlamp thingies?

MAI: Ah yes, that headlamp. That's very typical, innit?

PATRICIA: "Innit"? Innit? You're adopting some very Cockney expressions.

MAI: I'm learning from the best.

PATRICIA: How about making some sort of contraption that she could wear, if you wanted to make the doctor a Steampunk one?

MAI: That's a thought. Then I could have it for the Clockwork Alchemy convention! Yes yes! If she has some kind of tank on her back, with tubes coming out, she could be holding an injection gun, or a syringe to administer whatever concoction is brewing in the tank.

PATRICIA: Back in Queen Victoria's day, those quacks used to dream up all kinds of fancy names and properties for their elixirs. None of it was regulated back then of course, so they would use all kinds of dreadful ingredients, like arsenic and strychnine. They would claim all sorts of outrageous and miraculous properties for their potions. They could even say that the queen used it, never mind that it wasn't true. Let me send you some labels and you can perhaps draw your own version.

MAI: Thank you. How am I going to make the tank?

PATRICIA: You'll come up with something I'm sure. That said, it would be nice to see the liquid in there. A little glass vial?

MAI: Might be too fragile. Oh wait. Tap Plastics has these colored acrylic rods. I can use those.

PATRICIA: And the syringe?

MAI: I saw some metal and brass syringes on your Pinterest board. I can use small brass tubes. I'll give it a try anyway.

Dr. Von Klock
Elixir of Life Eternal
Elixir de Jouvence
Dr. Von Kl

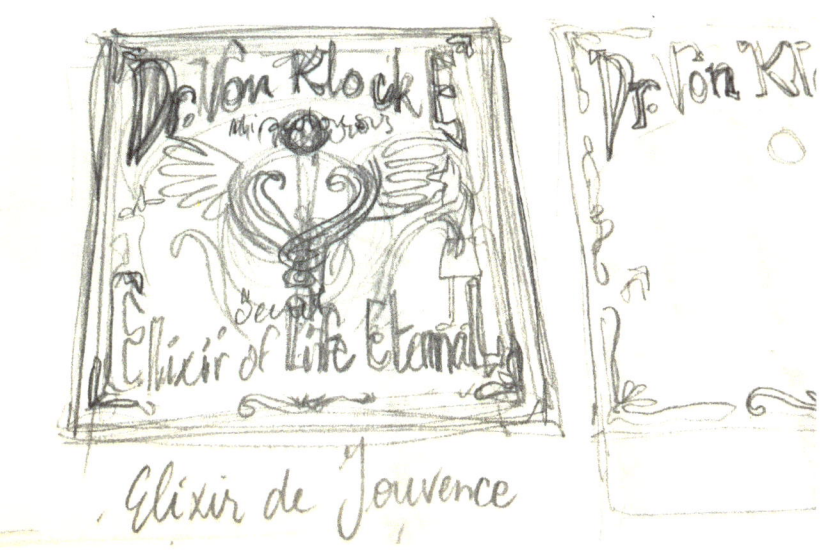

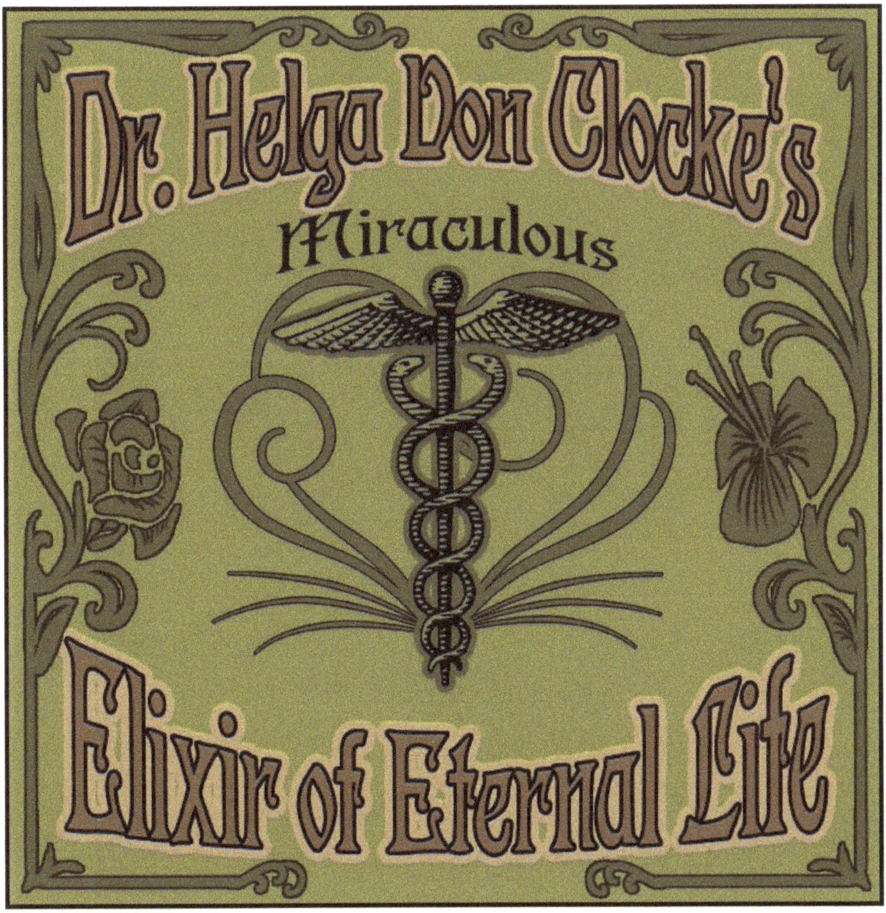
Dr. Helga Von Clocke's
Miraculous
Elixir of Eternal Life

Inga Von Clocke

Sherlock Holmes

Sherlock's Inverness coat was extremely challenging to make. Woven fabric frays, especially thick, woollen suiting fabric. I had to glue and iron all edges before sewing it together. Can you spot the paw print on the carpet pedestal?

Triumphs and Disasters

The title of this chapter was chosen by Patricia. She is something of a poetry nut and she told me that the phrase comes from a poem called "If" by the English poet Rudyard Kipling. This poem was not so long ago voted by the Brits as their favorite poem in a survey held by the BBC: "If you can meet with Triumph and Disaster/ And treat those two imposters just the same" is even inscribed above the player's entrance to the Centre (that's English for "Center") Court at Wimbledon.

I think the words serve well to illustrate my own list of taxidermical triumphs and disasters, because like I said before, both are equally valuable as a learning tool.

Attack of the Killer Moths

I begin with the absolute worst, which is not the way to go if you want to reserve the high dramatic note for the end of the chapter. I just want to get it out of the way, because it pains me to talk about it.

My most traumatic experience with regards to the meeces was the loss of several of them to moths.

I used to store my mice in cardboard boxes with separator inserts, which I believe are used for wine glasses. I could fit up to twelve of them in each box. Each mouse would be safe in its own tiny cubby. One box was mostly occupied by the Russells, a line that I created after doing a series of cowboys. We wanted to do a female counterpart to them. The Russells were inspired by Miss Kitty from the classic western TV series Gunsmoke. Miss Kitty Russell was the proprietor of the local saloon, and was played by the lovely Amanda Blake.

This is all relevant because of the long billowing skirt that she wore.

One day I happened to open the box housing the Miss Russells, and the face of one of them looked very strange and yellow. I picked it up and my brain couldn't comprehend what I was seeing. The face was just wrong, and it was horrifying! I looked at the arm, and half of it was in the same condition as the face, hairless and yellow. As I lifted up the skirt I finally spotted thin threads of silk stretching between the skin and the leather. I understood at once that the fur had been eaten by moth larvae. It had never occurred to me that mouse fur is like any other natural fiber, and is food to a moth's caterpillar just as wool is. The pests had laid their eggs under the leather skirt and upon hatching in the dark comfort of Miss Kitty's voluminous undergarments, the larvae had eaten their way up the mouse, leaving behind the yellow dried skin.

None of the mice in that box had escaped the infestation. I lost six mice to the little bastards. Several Miss Russells, a Volkova and a Mouseguard. I was heartbroken. Weeks of hard work had been gnawed beyond repair, and regardless of the labor, they are my precious babies!

I checked the other boxes thoroughly for any trace of the little worms, but luckily they had only infested that single one.

For months afterwards I had anxiety dreams in which I would find more little victims in other boxes. I would get up in the middle of the night to go check if the little ones were safe.

Needless to say, I switched from cardboard boxes to plastic containers with a proper lid, and I leave moth balls in them to keep the killers away. I'm pleased to report that there haven't been any more moth attacks since then.

The russels. R.I.P.

Conventions, Balls, and other such Events

It was a year after I started my journey into the enchanted world of taxidermy that I applied to be a vendor at an event.

The Edwardian Ball in San Francisco is held every winter at the Regency Theater on Van Ness Avenue. After the lovely lady at the squirrel taxidermy class recommended it as the perfect venue to sell my mice, I applied for a 6' table spot, and was accepted a few weeks later. I realized with a frisson of panic that I urgently had to come up with a proper way to display the mice, both the costume mice and the headmounts. Along with the display, which I hoped would match my mice both in quality and style, I also had to think of a proper way to wrap and pack them safely for customers to take home.

I had a couple of months to figure it all out. It wrote down a huge list of everything I could think of.

I signed up for a Square account, so I could swipe credit cards using my iPad mini.

I needed business cards, and I wanted little stickers carrying my logo. That's where my Photoshop skills came in handy, and moo.com printed them for me.

The packaging for the headmounts still eluded me. Thus far, I had shipped online orders simply wrapped in white tissue paper, inside a cardboard shipping box. I didn't like it, but I never came across anything of the proper size that could serve as a gift box. The boxes used for jewelry were usually flat, or long. The mouse heads had volume to them, including fragile, paper-thin ears, and I didn't want to risk crushing them.

One day, I went shopping at my favorite restaurant supply store. I needed to pick up plastic deli containers that I use frequently for cooking, as well as in my crafts. After placing them in my cart, I glanced across the aisle and I did a double take. There were stacks and stacks of plain white little Chinese take-out boxes, in all sizes. The clouds parted and the sun came through, shining down in a fanfare of golden trumpets.

Holy Chicken Chow Mein, Batman! I had found my packaging!

Boxes, stickers and business cards to sell headmounts at events.

I was very nervous on the days leading up to the Ball, which is very unlike me. I just had no idea what to expect. I had never worked in retail, ever.

In the end, it turns out I was very well prepared, except for my outfit. It turns out the ball is THE Victorian/ Edwardian/ Steampunk fashion event of the year. People spend months designing and working on their outfits, which include hats, undergarments, corsets, moustaches, makeup, headdresses, boots, Steampunk apparatus, lights and FX. If you're planning on attending both days, it's de rigueur to wear a different outfit on each evening. The resulting crowd is absolutely spectacular! Regrettably, I hadn't looked up pictures of the ball itself on the internet before attending, and I showed up just wearing a French striped shirt and a beret that was too big for me. Pitiful. Oh I was wearing pants as well. I thought I should mention it.

As I would later learn, when it comes to the outfits, "It's never too much". In other words, more is more.

Thankfully, even being grossly underdressed didn't spoil my first ball. I had a wonderful evening, two in fact, did really well, and I knew I would want to do more events, which I have done.

The truly wonderful thing about doing these events is that you get to witness people's reactions to the mice in person. I wasn't expecting such delight and glee as both men and women squealed with pure joy at the sight of my little characters.

First the glance, then the double-take as they realize that this is not the jewelry or apparel booth that they were expecting. They squint and frown as they try to figure out if these are real mice or fake ones. I nod and say "They're real mice!" Sometimes they frown some more in disbelief but they can't help but step up because they're seeing little people, and the costumes are so detailed that they cannot resist a closer look. I reiterate my claim by pointing out the whiskers and the teeth. The people smile, sometimes laugh out loud, and bring their hand to their mouth because they can't believe their eyes! They giggle. Their gaze travels from one mouse to the next, trying to take in all the details and they name each character out loud, to no-one in particular.

I will always remember this young woman, late in the evening. She was clearly intoxicated. Upon seeing the mice, she fell to her knees and started laughing, or crying perhaps, in front of my table. She kept squealing, "Oh my God they're so cute! SO CUTE! Oh my GOD!" She was sobbing and laughing at the same time, kneeling so she could observe the little creatures up close. Her friends had gathered around her and were laughing at her reaction. They apologized to me but by then I was laughing too. She'd had more than a few drinks obviously, but her response was so genuine, so unguarded, that her delight became contagious to everybody around the table.

Imagine two full days of that (though most people don't collapse in a full hysterical crisis), and you'll understand why I love doing events after long months isolated in the Leathery.

Although it reminds me that I spent a good part of the evening having to warn people "Watch out for your drink!" as they were either setting it down on my table or waving it around carelessly while pointing at the mice.

Doing events also gave me a chance to see who buys the mice. I thought it would give me an insight into who my customers are, and maybe do an attempt at marketing.

This is what I gathered:

Both genders and all ages are attracted to the mice.

Everybody will buy headmounts: teenagers, adults, grandparents, male or female, either for themselves or as a gift. They like the cuteness, the attention to details, the humorous reference to hunting trophies.

People who buy a full mouse are middle-aged or above, with enough of a disposable income to spend on art. The solo men who buy the mice tend to have a beard, but that might be because of the Steampunk genre.

Couples need to consult each other before bringing a dead animal into the house, so it's a two-part process: "Let me bring my husband over." People who do crafting or sewing themselves really appreciate the work that goes into my mice and will happily spend the money on them.

These things I noticed at all the events I have attended, but it brings me no closer to having a marketing target which I can use to spread the word.

Or rather, I suspect, marketing is not included in my skill set.

Opposite:
My first Edwardian Ball.,
At the California Academy of Sciences in San Francisco.

Jenny Lawson a.k.a. The Bloggess

My first celebrity encounter!

I vaguely remember someone mentioning Jenny Lawson in an email, or on Facebook, in regards to my mice. I didn't know who she was, so I looked her up. As you would discover too if you Googled Jenny Lawson, she's a very, very funny writer who maintains an extremely popular Blog, and she is the author of the best-seller book "Let's Pretend This Never Happened".

She collects taxidermy, especially odd vintage mounts. Her father was a taxidermist and she grew up surrounded by dead animals. Not unlike my own son right now...

I had been making mice only for a few months, and I was trying to figure out how to get the word out. I thought I could write to her and maybe she would mention my mice on her Blog. I composed a very short email with a picture of one of my mice and sent it into the ether.

Her assistant Mary replied the next day with a very brief email relaying Jenny's reaction, which was: "Holy shit I want those!"

Mary the Fairy Godmother and I corresponded for a while and we agreed to trade a graphic ad on her Blog for a mouse dressed up in Jenny's signature red dress. While I was working on it, Jenny's husband Victor picked up one of my mice at Paxton Gate as a birthday surprise. She ended up writing two posts about my mice.

The traffic to my website surged as a result, and converted into a few sales, but the conversion rate wasn't great. It made me realize that marketing is truly a science, because even though Jenny loves taxidermy, and her fans love reading about it, her readers aren't necessarily interested in buying and owning dead stuffed animals, however well done.

A year later, when her second book "Furiously Happy" came out, Jenny Lawson came to our local bookstore for a talk and a book signing event. I went and stood in the autograph line after her talk, and when my turn came, I introduced myself. After a second she looked up at me and exclaimed "I know who you are!" I gave her a little wrapped headmount to give to her lovely assistant Mary, since she had been so kind and helpful to me. Then we had our picture taken at the table. She had acquired more of my mice by then, and she told me she had shown them to her dad, who was the professional taxidermist in the family, and who, she said, approved of the work. One of the better specimens in her collection, apparently. Yay!

The Red Dress Mouse.

Fan Picture.

The Pet Snacks

When people see the headmounts, they immediately think they want one to hang over their cat's feeding bowl. And it would indeed be funny, except that, given half a chance, most cats will actually eat the head.

Several Etsy customers had to buy a second head because the first one had been eaten by their cat or dog. And who could resist such a treat? "Oooh, for ME?"

Some customers say they only had their back turned for a few seconds, but that's all it takes for a bite-size snack, especially for a puppy.

Now, whenever anyone purchases one of my headmounts, I add a note in the box to warn my customers about leaving the mice within reach of their pet, cat or dog.

Fortunately, nothing I use in making the head is toxic, although the headmounts do include a small screw to secure it to the escutcheon. But so far, no casualties.

For some reason, my cats have never tried to eat any of my mice. The old ones weren't hunters, and I've trained the new kitten to wait for me to feed him a couple of mice, once I've skinned them. He seems satisfied with the arrangement.

This headmount was chewed up by a customer's cat.

The Studio Visits

A few people who discovered via Etsy that I live in the same area as them have wanted to come visit my studio., or asked to pick up their order in person.

I always tell them that I work from my own house and wouldn't feel comfortable having strangers visit my home. Most of them understand and I'm able to ship their order by mail, as usual, and remain the semi-hermit I've become.

But I had to beat one particular person back with a stick to make them back off. First they inquired about coming over to visit my studio, which I declined. They then tried to convince me to meet for coffee and have a chat. I deflected. They just wouldn't take no for an answer. I always stay polite in my emails, but they really pushed it to the limit. I just had to stop answering their messages. They never even made a purchase!

Now I do love showing off my work in progress to my friends or even close acquaintances, and I can imagine that it would be fascinating to visit an art studio to see firsthand how it's done.

But simply living in the same city doesn't make a perfect stranger any less of a stranger, and I'm not about to give a guided tour of my home to anyone just off the street.

The age of the Internet has spawned some very strange assumptions when it comes to social boundaries...

On the other side of that particular coin however, is the fact that were it not for the Internet, then Patricia and I would never have met.

Patricia and me on Skype.

The Buzzfeed Article

On December 7th 2016, I noticed a huge spike in traffic on my Etsy store, and after checking the stats, discovered that buzzfeed.com had just published an article called "19 Stocking Stuffers Your Kids Will Like More Than Their Presents". My brand new mouselopes were featured at #15, and the blurb contained a direct hyperlink to my listing. You could tell from the comments that people were, justifiably, a little shocked. Taxidermy for kids? Really?

Regardless, in a few hours, I was sold out of not only the mouselopes, but of my entire Christmas inventory of headmounts. And it was only the beginning of December!

That evening, I enlisted the help of my wife and our son's piano teacher to pack up and label all the orders. For two days my Etsy store was empty, and people were enquiring about the sold-out headmounts. Everybody around me was begging me to list something, anything, even a pre-sale. I felt like it was cheating, but in the end, I listed a pre-sale for 20 mouselopes, to be shipped the following week. They were sold out that day.

The problem with taxidermy is that it requires some time to dry, and you can double that time during the cold winter months, even in the mild weather of the Bay Area. A week turnaroud is very, very optimistic.

So I invested a day building a tray caddy so I could stack trays of heads, and I bought a reptile heat lamp to accelerate the drying process. It was also very convenient to speed-thaw the frozen mice.

Thanks to the tray caddy, I could make loads of heads in advance, and while they dried with the help of the heat lamp, I would work on the escutcheons.

Thanks to the heat lamp I managed to ship the Mouselopes early, and I spent the next three weeks constantly trying to catch up with the orders. When I would finish and list a batch of ovals, the shields would run out. I would make more shields, then the mouselopes would sell out again.

I would show up every day at our local Post Office with a dozen of the same cube boxes, sometimes twice a day.

Christmas finally came and went and then it was all back to a normal, slow pace.

Since then, thanks to the tray caddy, I always have heads ready to be mounted, so that I can better manage the different variations of headmounts and be ready when shortages occur.

The thing is, every year before Christmas, I am confident I have enough inventory, but I am always thoroughly under-prepared for the holiday surge. I end up spending the whole month of December hustling to make more as they sell, managing and packing orders at the same time. I subsequently tell myself that I should really spend the rest of the year making heads like crazy. Except that when the slow season settles in, between March/July, I lose the pressure to make more, so I decide I'll be fine. I'll never learn…

Even now, as I'm writing this and it's almost July, I know I should be hard at work making heads, but I'm not. "In a minute…", as Patricia would say.

Mouselopes.

My tray caddy.

Henri Souris

I can't remember exactly how Henri came about. I believe it was the result of a discussion between Diane and me. We came up with the idea of a French looking mouse, not for sale, but that we could take with us on our travels. When we found ourselves in an interesting place, we could take pictures of him, as if he was a real person. As I mentioned earlier I was born and raised in France, and I go back every other year to see my family. My sister makes the reverse trip on the off-years. Our son Victor and his French cousins get to spend time together, making so much noise that we get complaints from the Space Station, and when we're all on this side of the herring pond, we usually go on a week-long road trip in the minivan. It provides plenty of photographic opportunities. Besides, we live in the San Francisco Bay Area, which is exceedingly beautiful and full of fantastic spots for a picture, any time of the year. It's easy to take it for granted when you see it every day, but people travel from across the world to come visit!

I made a French looking mouse with a stripey shirt, a black beret and a moustache. I named him Henri, with an i not a y, and Souris is the French word for mouse. It's also the French word for smile.

We are currently in the reign of Henri III, with Henri the First living in Paris with my friend Sophie, and Henri II living with my sister and her family in Bouc-Bel-Air, in the south of France.

You can follow Henri's travels on my Instagram: @leheartdesign.

Henri Souris in Paris.

Henri I in front of Notre Dame de Paris.

Henri II with coquelicots in the south of France.

Henri III and the Golden Gate Bridge.

Henry III and me at the Clockwork Alchemy convention in San Jose.

The Art Deco Lamp

The strangest payment I have ever accepted was a trade for a headmount on Etsy. The person couldn't afford the price, but offered to send a beautiful Art Deco lamp as payment. I even received detailed photographs. I admit I wasn't too keen, and didn't understand the reasoning. I tried to talk her out of it, not least because the shipping alone would pay for half of the head! Besides, I had absolutely no use for a lamp. Patricia loves Art Deco, but the cost of shipping the heavy lamp to England would have been prohibitive.

The buyer wouldn't give up though, so I sent a headmount and received a lamp in return.

It's still in its box in the garage. I'll never do that again...

Geoff Vassallo

Geoff, the wonderful teacher of my first Paxton Gate taxidermy class, also taught the squirrel class I took more recently when I thought I might dress up squirrels instead of mice.

People tend not to notice me in a class situation. I have what is known as a resting bitch face, I don't require much attention or extra help: I pay attention, I'm a fast learner, I do what I'm required to do without a fuss and I don't talk much. I'm in and out like a thief in the night.

At the end of 2016, Geoff contacted some of his students to check on his mailing list, and politely asked how we were doing, and if we had any taxidermy projects to show him, and to please send pictures.

So I did, and I think he was impressed with how far I'd gone after the classes.

He asked if he could come visit my studio. I did hesitate, because at that point he was little more than a stranger. Who didn't even live in the same town! However, since he did help change my life after all, I agreed and sent him my address.

He came the following night after teaching a class at Paxton Gate, and we were like two puppies meeting for the first time. He gushed over my mice, which is always nice from anyone but was especially nice coming from the master himself.

Most of the new techniques I had come up with didn't strike me as being especially innovative or clever. They were mostly designed to save me time and produce consistent shapes. But Geoff seemed most impressed and wasn't shy to ask about them. I was more than happy to share, and return some of the knowledge he had passed on to me.

Isn't it everyone's fantasy to return and impress their teacher? Done it!

Regrettably, I don't even have a selfie with him...

The Rehydrating Mice

In December of 2015, when I was still doing my first round of selling in person at various events, a young woman from the Fairfax Farmers' Market contacted me to inquire if I would be interested in being a vendor with them.

After due consideration, Diane and I decided to give it a shot.

Since it was an outdoor market, I invested in a 10'x10' canopy, to keep the mice (and me) safe from the elements. The weather forecast was predicting a cold, possibly rainy weekend. The canopy came with a possible three walls, a front flap, and an awning over the front. I was planning on definitely using the back wall.

The day dawned, a Saturday. It was cold, overcast, with a light, steady rain. We could have cancelled. Exposing preserved mice to the damp open air is not ideal, and I was sure the event organizer would have understood.

But I wanted to give it a go. It was right before Chrismas, and it was a new venue to try.

My wife and I packed up the minivan and drove the 20 minutes to Fairfax. By the time we got there, it was raining properly. We setup the canopy, including walls and awning, and secured the four poles with sandbags, as recommended in the user manual. It wasn't too windy, but better safe than sorry.

By the time everybody was set up, there couldn't have been more than 10 vendors there, all of us huddled in a circle. A lot of the other vendors hadn't shown up because of the weather.

Nevertheless, once settled in, we were having a good time. The vendors who were there were thoroughly friendly and fun. The one thing I really love about being a vendor is the sense of community. We sampled a lot of good foods, since the rain had kept most shoppers at home and vendors weren't terribly busy. We had soup, pastries, bread, cheese and wonderful middle eastern specialities.

I was even less busy than the food booths. Nobody really expects taxidermy at a farmer's market. I don't think I sold anything, but I still got a few squeals.

About two hours in I was re-arranging the headmounts on the display, as you do when there's not much going on, and I happened to touch a mouse's ear with my finger. To my horror, it was soft. I checked the full mice. All their ears were supple, as if the mice were alive again.

Even though we were under the cover of the canopy, my mice were rehydrating from the damp weather!

We ran to see the organizer, told her about the situation, and we packed up everything in a hurry.

Once home, I laid out all the meeces and headmounts on the dining table and cranked up the heating in the house.

I never went back. Never did an outdoor event again.

We thought the mice would be safe from the damp under the canopy.

Julius Cesar commission. The draping of the fabric required a lot of ironing in place with a small curling iron.

Julius Musculus. The surname (it means last name) Musculus is deceiving. In Latin, it doesn't mean "muscular" or "strong", it means "mouse".

A Day in the Life II

PATRICIA: I was watching the Edinburgh Military Tattoo on the telly last night. I always enjoy it.

MAI: I thought you hated tattoos.

PATRICIA: Not that kind of tattoo, bozo. It's a big spectacular military music and marching event that takes place every year on the esplanade of Edinburgh Castle. They have military bands from all over the world as well as the Scottish pipes and drums.

MAI: I just found a video on YouTube. It certainly looks spectacular!

PATRICIA: It really is ma bonny wee lassie. Och aye the noo.

MAI: I need subtitles babe.

PATRICIA: Oh ha-bloody-ha... Now, what about a Scottish mouse? In full regalia?

MAI: Ooooh! With little bagpipes?

PATRICIA: Brilliant! And with his own clan tartan?

MAI: What's that, the kilt?

PATRICIA: Each Scottish clan is entitled to wear its own particular plaid pattern, called a tartan. That's why their kilts are all in a different color and pattern. The kilt-makers use 24 feet of fabric to make an authentic Scottish kilt! It's because of the way it's pleated in the back. Must weigh a ton....

MAI: Oh poo! You know what? I'll never find a plaid fabric with the pattern scaled down small enough for a mouse, especially if what you say about the tartans is true.

PATRICIA: Of course it's true! Can you paint it yourself?

MAI: It should be woven, no? Let me look online.

PATRICIA: I just sent you a map of Scotland showing each clan by area so you can pick which one you want to make by name.

MAI: Ooh, our friend Sheila's name is MacIntosh. We could call the mice MacIntosh. I wonder what their tartan looks like.

PATRICIA: It will be on the map I sent. I forgot to say that each clan also has its own crest with a motto. The MacIntosh motto is... let me find it... hang on... the crest has a cat on it. "Touch Not The Cat Bot A Glove".

MAI: What does that mean?

PATRICIA: Don't touch this cat without a glove, or words to that effect.

MAI: Oh my god! Don't touch this cat... isn't it perfect for a mouse??

PATRICIA: Indeed!

MAI: I'm looking at fabrics for miniatures on eBay. They do have plaid patterns. I might order a few, and we'll see if any of them match, even just a little bit.

PATRICIA: How are you going to make the bagpipes?

MAI: I have no idea. I have to look at how they're made in real life. They probably have rules too.

PATRICIA: Undoubtedly. I'll get you some info. You'll also have to do the sporran.

MAI: Sporran? What's that?

PATRICIA: It's a little purse that hangs in front of their bits. To hold their essentials I suppose. You know, cab fare, lippy, tissues…

MAI: Ha! It sounds weird. Send me some pictures.

PATRICIA: Also, the socks and how they wear them is very specific.

MAI: No no, no socks. I can't do socks. No pants, no socks, no shoes.

PATRICIA: I know, I just had to mention it. I'll send you pictures and you can decide later…

Margotte and Shrewbert Le Swain
I loved sculpting and painting the pet snail. The shell is real though...

La crème de la crème

I'm very picky about the designs I choose to make. Over the years, I've heard hundreds of suggestions from various people about this character or that. I stare at them in silence, and they usually apologize for being so bold, but I'm not giving them the evil eye, I'm actually thinking about it. I would never reject something outright, even though I do end up rejecting most ideas, for very valid reasons.

The main reason for rejection is when the outfit isn't immediately recognizable. When you first see the mouse, you need to know right away who the mouse represents. With the characters losing their facial features and hair in favor of a mouse, the only way to recognize them is the outfit. Jane Austen created lovely characters, but unless you read the name, the costumes don't tell you much. Same with Dickens, or a lot of movie characters. Diane suggested drag queens, but how would you know that it's a boy impersonating a girl when you can't tell it's a boy to begin with?

Darth Vader, super heroes or other mask-wearing characters don't work, because if they wear a mask, what's the point of having a mouse underneath?

Other characters I stay away from include any design that might remind people that the mouse is dead. I work very hard to give my mice very lively features and dynamic poses, so they look alive. People find the mice enchanting because they look like they're real characters, not just mangled corpses, contrived into an unnatural pose by wires and stuffing.

It means no zombies, Frankenstein creatures, mummies, Phantom of the Opera, characters with injuries, blood or large scars.

Ideally, a character should have an iconic outfit, with equally iconic and immediately recognizable accessories or attributes that can be used in its design. The additional limitation is that I don't do pants or shoes.

A Roman soldier, Sherlock Holmes, Dracula, safari hunters, Napoleon, witches, a cowboy, the Queen of Hearts; they seem simple and obvious when you look at them, but a lot of thought goes into the choice of colors, accessories, stance and pedestal, so people can identify them at first glance, if not by name, by archetype.

Regardless of the design, I always have fun with it, and there are little secrets that you probably would never notice, even if you own one of my mice. One of them is that I include little magnets inside the clay head so that the hats actually clip on and can be removed. I didn't like gluing the hats onto the fur, so after the first few mice, I came up with this much more elegant solution to keep their hat on without any glue. Also, there is a treasure in every little bag when the outfit includes a bag. Swords can be unsheathed, guns fit in their holster, and there are quotes inscribed inside the books.

Here are a few mice that I'm particularly proud of, or found interesting to work on:

Safari Hunters

These British explorers came after the first series, the Judds. Patricia named them the Brocklebanks. They're posh, you see.

Real life pith helmets were originally made out of pith, a plant material. It's lightweight, breathable and almost white, to keep you cool.

The uniforms came in white, but back in the olden days people would dye the fabric to a light tan by soaking it in strong tea.

I sculpted a pith helmet shape out of Sculpey and molded light glove leather over it, then glued it at the seams. I secured the edges together with a strip of thin leather, and glued a round "button" at the very top.

I stained the white leather with strong tea for the jacket. It does give it a nice, subtle shade of brown that's much more pleasant than a glaring white.

The first series came equipped with cameras for the gents and binoculars for the ladies. I didn't like the ideas of guns at the time, so Patricia and I settled on these peaceful accessories. For the camera, I started with a little cube of aluminium (which is the "proper" way of saying aluminum, which is missing the i. Patricia has scolded me numerous times for not saying it the European way), cut out of an aluminium rod, and I dismantled a few broken electronic devices to gather tiny interesting metal shapes to glue onto it.

I made a second series called the Winterbournes. This time I gave them rifles. I ground down a tiny piece of teak for the rifle's stock, dyed and varnished it, then glued on a little brass rod for the barrel. Again, I used miscellaneous electronics and clock mechanism parts to complete the details.

No two cameras or rifles are the same, since I made them all from found objects.

Gnomes

This series is special in a lot of ways.

First, every gnome I made is different. Pose, activity, accessories, colors. Every single one presented a new challenge, whether it was designing it, the making of the accessories, or the names.

The common characteristics were no walk in the park either: I had to make boots, whereas I had never made pants or shoes before. Each gnome also had to have a beard, and a long, wonky, pointy hat.

And I had to make a trout.

Patricia and I decided to make garden gnomes around Christmas. They would all have different activities. We deliberately left things a bit vague, because each gnome's accessory would depend on whether I was able to make them or not.

I had gathered a few snail shells, I could make a snail pet on a leash.

A pickaxe, a book and a pair of glasses, a wooden pitcher, a wheelbarrow, check.

A fishing rod; tricky because of the reel, but I figured it out. Check.

The names, for once, had to be entirely made up. I knew from playing role-playing games that gnomes have very whimsical, funny names. It was hard to explain to Patricia, so I turned to my game master Chris and sent him a text. In two seconds, he gave me five names.

I forwarded the names to Patricia, who was at the time confined to her apartment with an injured foot. She threw herself wholeheartedly into the name game. She immersed herself into the concept and came up with a huge list, way more than I would ever need, just to take her mind off her poorly foot.

"What about a trout hanging on the fishing rod, love?", Patricia asked.

"The fishing rod with the reel is enough, innit? How would I make a trout?", I protested.

"With Sculpey, like you do."

"It would have to be all shimmery and shiny. I don't think it needs it."

"I just think a trout would be splendid. That poor gnome came back empty handed from his fishing trip. But don't listen to your daft old bat. I'm only here to make suggestions..."

So I made a trout out of polymer clay and it looks splendid!

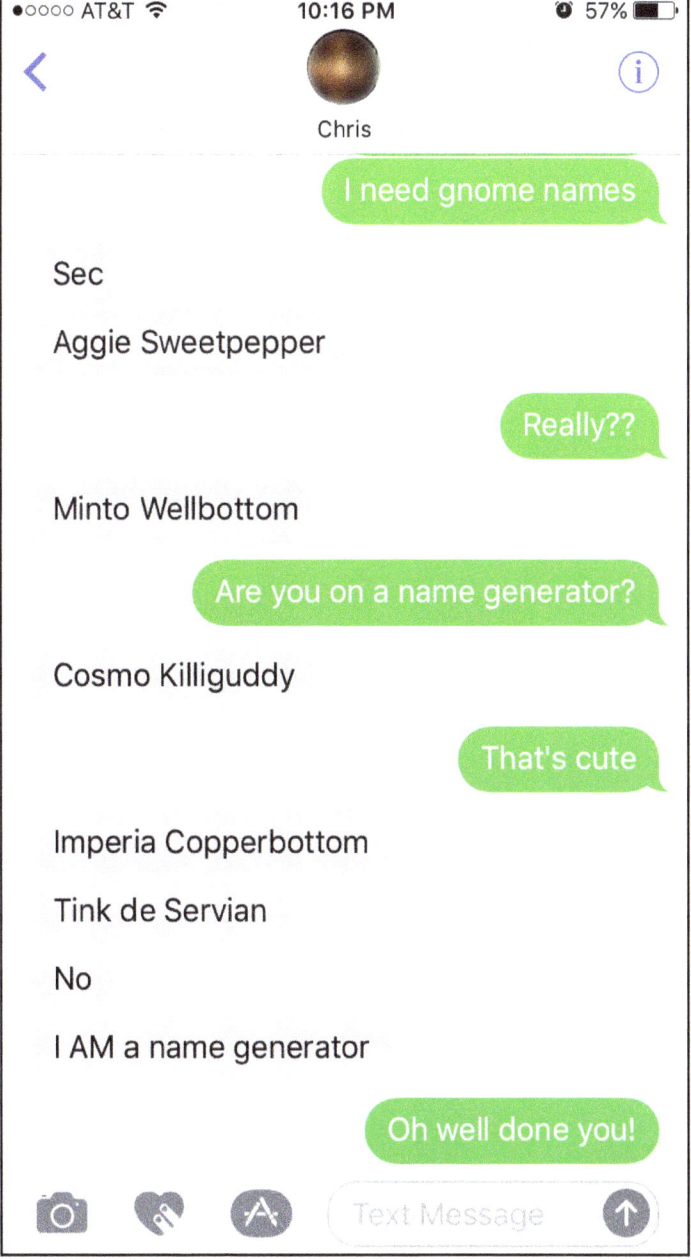

A splendid trout, that is!

Grim Reapers

The Grim Reapers started as a Gorey Mouse. Edward St. John Gorey was an American writer and artist who gained a cult following for his illustrations, which are mostly black and white. They are also wonderfully funny and macabre. I wanted to make Edward Gorey mouses for my first Edwardian Ball, since the Ball is named both for King Edward VII and Edward Gorey.

After going through his work, Patricia and I decided to give a sleek black mouse a pair of black wings, a black coat and a black top hat. No accessories, just a clean silhouette. Picking names was tricky. In the end, we came up with synonyms of darkness: Bleak, Darkness, Stygian, Tenebris and Umbra.

I had to wet-mold the wings out of leather, over two (mostly) symmetrical Sculpey shapes, then add them into the armature as an extra pair of limbs.

They were hugely popular, so much so that I made another series that were explicitly Grim Reaper. They each wielded a scythe and we named them Pestilence, Drought, Disease, Deluge and Famine.

The third series were each armed with a large knife, and we called them the Grim Rippers. Get it?

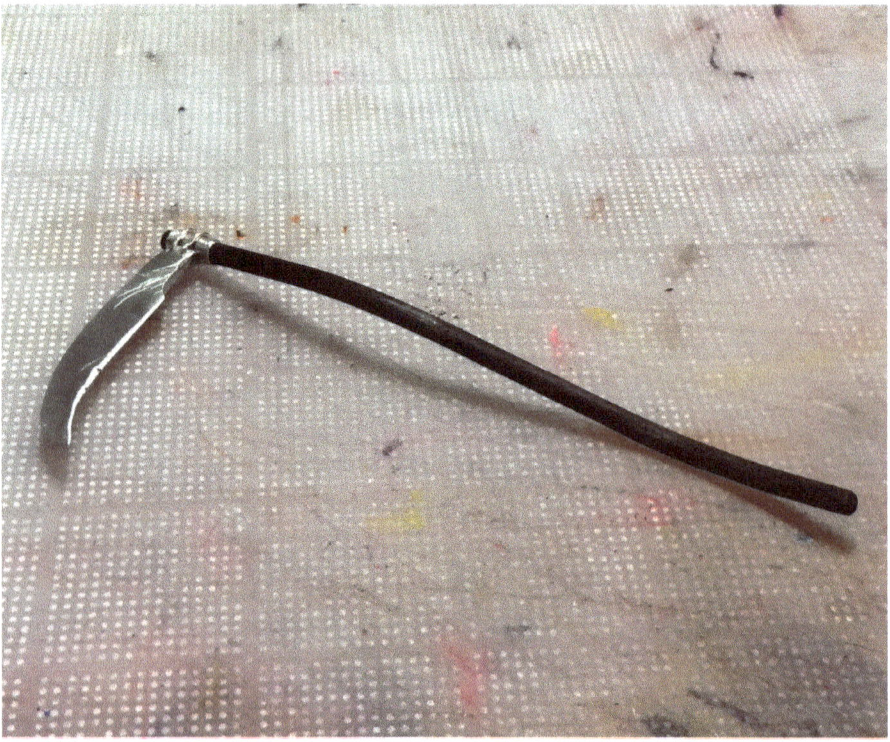

Little Red Riding Hood

Little Red was initially a commission. I really liked the idea, and after a little research, we found out it was initially published in France (my people!). We decided we would give her a basket with bread in one hand, and a lantern with a candle in the other, so she could find her way through the dark forest.

It was a lot of work because I had to weave the basket and make (and bake!) the bread out of polymer clay, and then make the lantern. However, it turned out so well that in addition to the commission, I made four more to make a complete series. I mounted the first four on a wooden square as usual, but kept one aside for myself. I had this idea to make a diorama with it.

A few weeks later, I set off to make a little forest perched on top of a leather-bound book. To make the terrain and the book, I made papier maché for the first time in my life. I collected sawdust and dyed it brown and green for the soil and grass. The trees were made of real branches with glued-on plastic leaves that I plucked from pre-made craft store bushes. Out of Sculpey, I made snails coming out of real miniature snail shells, a toad and clusters of mushrooms. I completed the book by covering it in real leather and tooling the title in French on the spine.

It took me about three weeks to complete.

Mad Hatter

I had made a series of Queen of Hearts, which are fabulous and I don't remember why I didn't consider the Mad Hatter first. I think I didn't know how to approach it, and what accessories to give him.

In researching the classic John Tenniel illustrations for the Queen, we had gathered some Mad Hatter reference as well, and once we'd had a good think, we came up with the stacked teacups and tea pot, and he would be standing on a white tablecloth with tea stain rings on it.

I wanted him to look mad and happy. I had made open mouths for the Draculs already, so I revisited that idea, with a smile on top.

This time, instead of painting the inside of the mouth and tongue after sculpting it, I used colored Sculpey directly, with much cleaner results.

I also made the teacups, saucers and teapot out of white polymer clay, and painted the tiny decorations on them.

The hat is slightly oversized, and is adorned with various hatpins, feathers and a bow as well as the iconic price tag.

The resulting Mad Hatter is just a joy to behold. He's so mad, and so happy! This was also the first time I had tried a very dynamic stance, and it completely brought him to life! Definitely one of my favorites. Patricia's too. I ended up making three series so far, all in different colors: first green, then purple and orange for the latest series.

Supreme Court Justice Ruth Bader Ginsburg

By far the most unexpected and interesting commission.

I usually don't do hair, but this mouse required a little bun at the back of her head.

I fashioned a leather-bound book of the Constitution, rather than a scroll.

I hand-burned the seal of the Supreme Court on the pedestal, and added her famous nickname "Notorious RBG" on the front.

I think the end result actually looks like her.

Out of all the tributes she receives, I bet she wouldn't expect to be immortalized in a mouse!

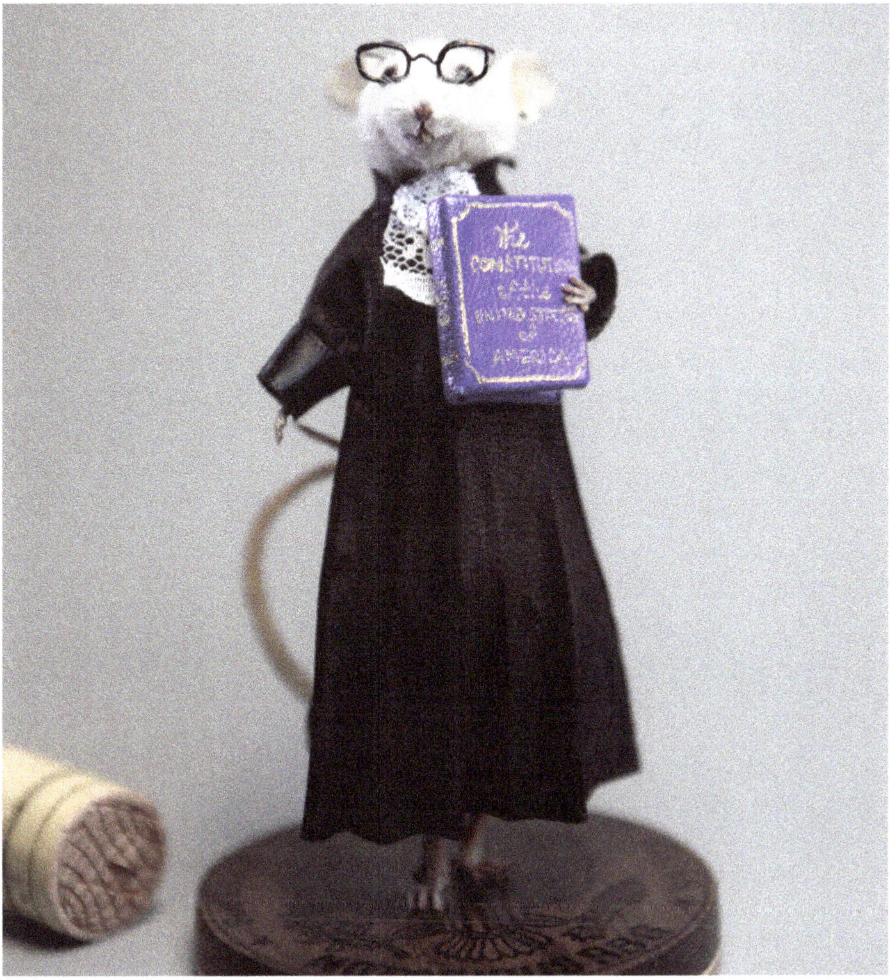
CONSTITUTION
UNITED STATES
AMERICA

STATES
NOTORIOUS RBG

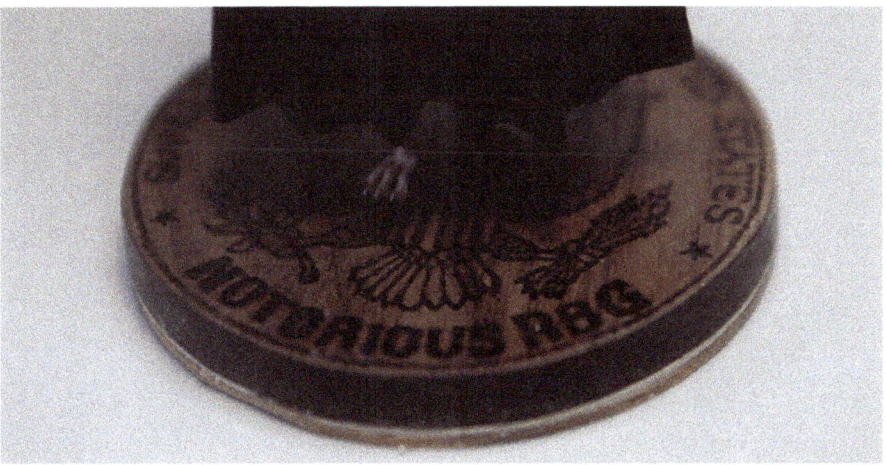

Mouseguard

When I'm at events, everybody mentions the movie "Dinner for Schmucks", which features a number of taxidermy mouse/hamster dioramas at the end. I haven't seen the whole movie, but the diorama scene is on YouTube.

People also ask about Red Wall and Mouseguard, both graphic novels featuring anthropomorphized mice.

While at an event in San Jose, someone ordered a custom mouse from Mouseguard. We researched it, and I really liked the classic fantasy style. The drawing style had the mice characters more squat, with chubby bodies and small eyes, which I tried to match.

I asked David Petersen, the author, for permission and he granted it, so I made a series of five. One went to the person who ordered it, one to David Petersen, two sold and the last one was killed by the moths.

The Log Lady

Throwback to the 90's! This commission made me smile. I remember living in Paris and watching "Twin Peaks" with my boyfriend and his roommate on TV every week. David Lynch's TV series was so weird and different. My boyfriend's roommate was attending film school, so we even rented "Eraserhead", which was difficult to watch but… interesting.

Anyway, someone wanted a Log Lady mouse. I accepted the challenge.

And a challenge it was.

At the beginning, I had used leather because that's what I had used to make the armor. It turns out it had been a judicious choice, because it's very easy to work with. You can dye it any color you want, it doesn't fray, you can glue it or sew it, glue things onto it; you can stretch it, shape it and it doesn't tear easily.

Every piece of clothing that the Log Lady wears is knit or fabric. With patterns. I found out that it's really hard to find patterns in a scale small enough for mice.

Working small with suiting fabric and knits was hard work. I spent a lot of time with a tiny iron, hemming or shaping the clothes, then sewing them together, burning and cutting the fraying fibers as they threatened to unravel.

It's too bad none of the other characters in "Twin Peaks" have such a recognizable outfit, or I would have done an ensemble cast.

Harry Potter

Another commission.

As you have probably ascertained by now, I don't usually do pop culture characters. I don't mind commissions if they are appropriate for a mouse and interesting, but I would rather we design something ourselves, Patricia and I.

This customer initially wanted Harry Potter flying on his broom, which I couldn't figure out how to mount. They had to settle for Harry with the Nimbus in one hand and pointing his wand in the other, standing on a pedestal reminiscent of a grimoire. He even has the scar on his forehead, although it doesn't show on any of the pictures I took.

Despite the pose change, I think my customer was delighted with the result.

Carmen Miranda

Carmen was a brilliant suggestion from Patricia. Though I had heard of her, I wasn't familiar with the accomplishments of this Brazilian entertainer. But the idea of a sexy, bare midriff and a huge, colorful fruit-filled headdress was wonderful.

Gathering reference made us realize that the headdresses were actually very stylish and elaborate, as opposed to the caricatures we see on the pre-packaged Carmen Miranda costumes at the Halloween stores. Some had flowers, some butterflies, each design was very refined and elaborate. It turns out Carmen herself had worked as a hat maker back in Brazil. Not too shabby!

Again, finding patterns and ribbons at the right scale was tricky, and every dress I made is a different color, with different trims. The pink one, which is still available, has really wonky eyes and I laugh every time I see her. I don't think she's suitable to be for sale, but you never know… I've seen worse.

Miss Havisham

Ah, Miss Havisham. One of my masterpieces that almost didn't happen.

At the 2017 Edwardian Ball, my neighbor's booth was called Miss Havisham's Curiosities. This husband and wife team were lovely neighbors, and they wore fantastic outfits! Melissa, the wife, bought a Dracul on the first night. The next day, she asked if I had ever considered making Dickens characters, in particular Miss Havisham. I apologized for not knowing who she was, and she explained the character to me. She's from "Great Expectations", and had been left at the altar by her groom many years prior. Her house is still filled with all the wedding decorations, the whole table setting, including the rotting wedding cake. Of course Patricia knew who she was, and thought it would make a great mouse.

At this point I'd had to turn down some commissions because I was taking 3D modeling contract work regularly, which brought in ten times more money than a mouse would for the same amount of time. But Miss Havisham grew on me once Patricia gave me the whole story, and she finally convinced me. After the ball, I had one free week before starting on a new freelance job, so I hustled and made her in a few days.

I made the flowers out of fabric, and burned the edges of her tattered wedding dress with my little soldering iron. I used gray, iridescent glass beads for the eyes, which gave her this ghostly, slightly absent look. I brushed white pastel powder over her bouquet and crown as if dust and time had faded the colors over the years.

The wedding cake pedestal, which I first resisted, is made out of white Sculpey wrapped over rounds of wood and aluminium foil. There is even a tiny mouse (!) gnawing on it.

I want to make her into a series one day.

Miss Havisham

Hector Brocklebank.
I made Hector in the winter of 2017 for composer Michael Giacchino.

Olga Volkova
She's dressed in a real lamb's wool coat and hat. I found out I'm allergic to wool while working on it with a mini electric groomer, scattering tiny pieces of fur all over my desk to trim it down to the right length.

A Day in the Life III

MAI: I thought about the Henri VIII idea but it's still too intimidating for me. People really liked the Little Red Riding Hood. Maybe we can continue with fairy tales, or classic literature characters. How about the Queen of Hearts? She fits the bill.

PATRICIA: Would you include the playing card, à la classic Tenniel illustration?

MAI: We can design it as we want, a mix between Tenniel and our own. Corset of course, crown, lots of hearts, scepter and a regal dress…

PATRICIA: I think it's a super idea.

MAI: I will probably have to make the heart shapes and patterns by hand. I will never find fabric with hearts that small. Let me look if I can find stamps at least.

PATRICIA: Tenniel used the playing card design for her dress. If you don't want to do that, we could use it on the pedestal or as a backdrop.

MAI: Too bad I can't make the army of cards. It would be fun, but that's too many mice.

PATRICIA: How about the croquet game? You could have her holding the flamingo.

MAI: Oh yes! But we could also do the "Off with her head" pose, pointing.

PATRICIA: You could do 3 of this and 2 of that.

MAI: I like it! Was the Tenniel croquet ball a hedgehog too? Like the Disney one?

PATRICIA: I believe it was, but let me send you some references.

MAI: Reference.

PATRICIA: References. Plural.

MAI: Isn't references when you look for a job and you need people to refer you? In games when we look for reference it's singular. Like research. You don't say researches.

PATRICIA: We say references.

MAI: We say reference.

PATRICIA: You say it wrong. But it's your mice, you say it however you want.

MAI: Ah! I found some small heart-shaped leather punches. And they're shipping from California, so they should be here pretty fast. Boop! Ordered!

PATRICIA: Splendid! And Tenniel had indeed a hedgehog as a ball in his illustrations. Are you going to make one?

MAI: Maybe. Though I don't like having something on the pedestal. Maybe she can hold it.

PATRICIA: Or she can hold the flamingo with both hands, as if about to strike.

MAI: That would be a better pose, more dynamic.

PATRICIA: Well then. We don't need a ball after all.

MAI: I can start on the crown. I have some brass tubing, it should work as a start. The Disney one was very simple, I think we could do something more elaborate.

PATRICIA: Look at Saint Edward's Crown. It has the arches.

MAI: Isn't it funny that I always have to start on the hat, when it's the thing that I could keep for last, even after I do the mouse?

PATRICIA: You have always done it this way.

MAI: I feel like the hat makes the character. Once that's settled, I can move forward with the rest of the costume.

PATRICIA: If the hat fits…

MAI: If the crown fits…

PATRICIA: It's a Queen!

A Day in the Life III

The Queen of Hearts: "Off with her head!"

At Last, Taxidermy Instructions

Here I present a step-by-step guide of the whole taxidermy process.

I applied some of the techniques I learned in the Paxton Gate taxidermy classes to my mice, with a fair degree of success. My methods have evolved quite a bit since I started, and both my skills and productivity have improved through practice. Yours will too.

If you are planning on dressing up the mouse, have the costume and accessories ready before you proceed to the taxidermy part. It is much easier to put on clothes and adjust the fit while you can still move the limbs and head. Once the mouse is dry, you would have to dress a rigid body, and the stance might not be right anymore after you've added the outfit and accessories.

Back in 2015, I produced and uploaded a tutorial video on YouTube, and I suggest you watch it as a companion to this set of instructions. It should come up if you search for "Mouse taxidermy tutorial by Le Heart Design". Note that the video has been age-restricted and you need to be logged in to access it.

Procuring the mouse

The good news is you don't have to kill a mouse to embark upon this adventure. You should be able to go to any pet store that sells reptiles and buy a frozen feeder mouse. Look at the sizes they offer and pick one that you like. I use the large adult size. If you're able to, make sure the ears aren't torn and that there are no bald patches or visible injuries. These things don't matter if you're feeding it to a snake, but a mouse with a mangled ear won't look quite right when it's preserved for posterity.

The cost should be no more than a few dollars, and if this is your first mouse, pick a white one. It makes it easier to see and to skin. As you gain more experience, you can start preserving colored mice too. It's just a little more difficult to distinguish between the skin and flesh when working on it.

If somehow you came in possession of a dead, wild mouse, or any other wild rodent, put it in a plastic bag and in the freezer for a few days. It will kill fleas and other unwanted parasites. Personally, I still wouldn't trust it, which is why I buy mine.

Supplies

Besides the mouse, here's what you'll need:

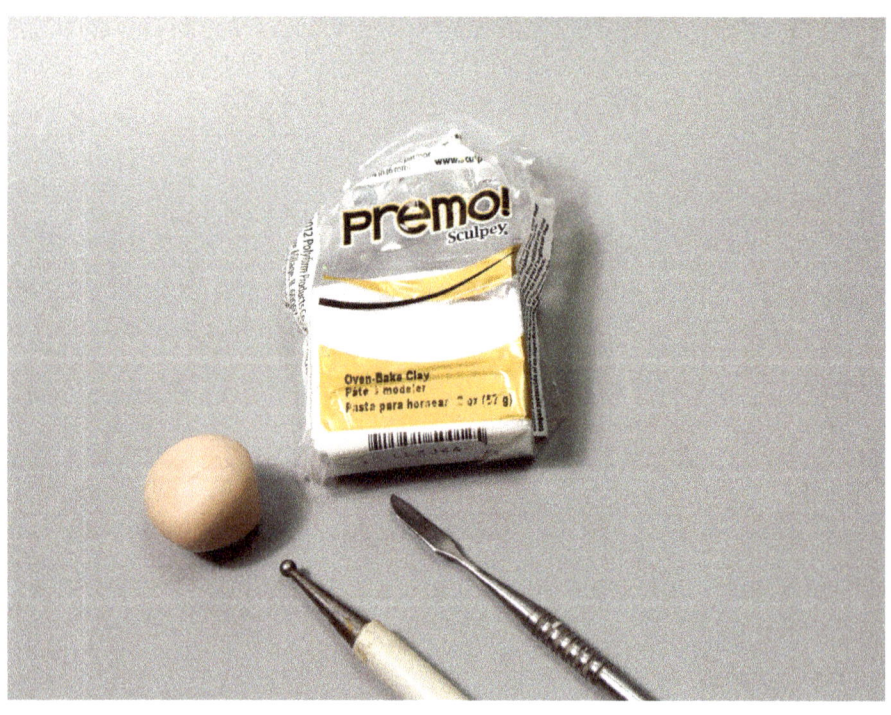

A little piece of beige or white polymer clay, and whatever sculpting tools you have available.

Two black beads 6/0 size E for the eyes, or 4mm if you find round beads without a hole.

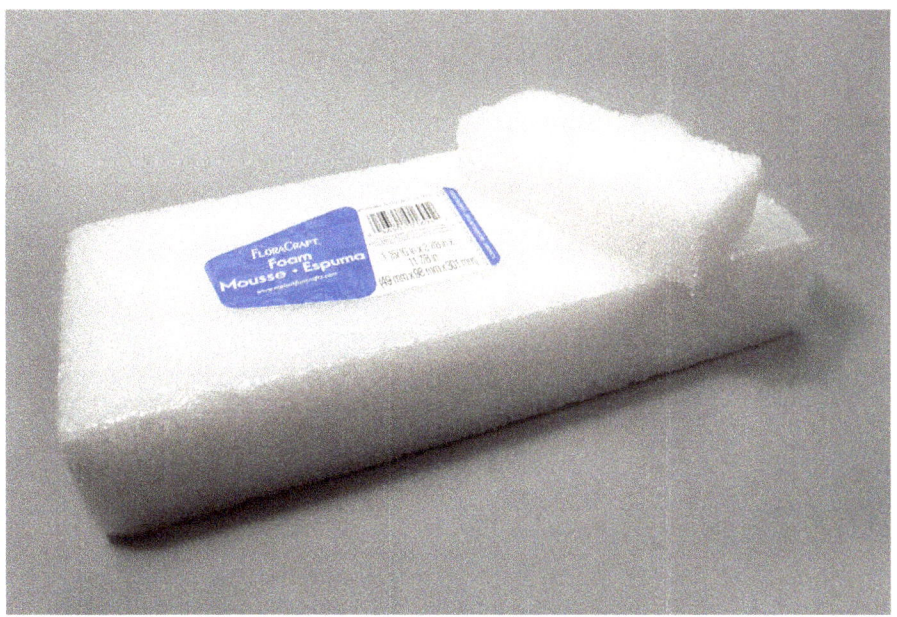

White polyurethane foam from the flower arrangement section of the craft store.

A coarse rasp and sandpaper.

White sewing thread (the color of the mouse you picked) and a smallish needle.

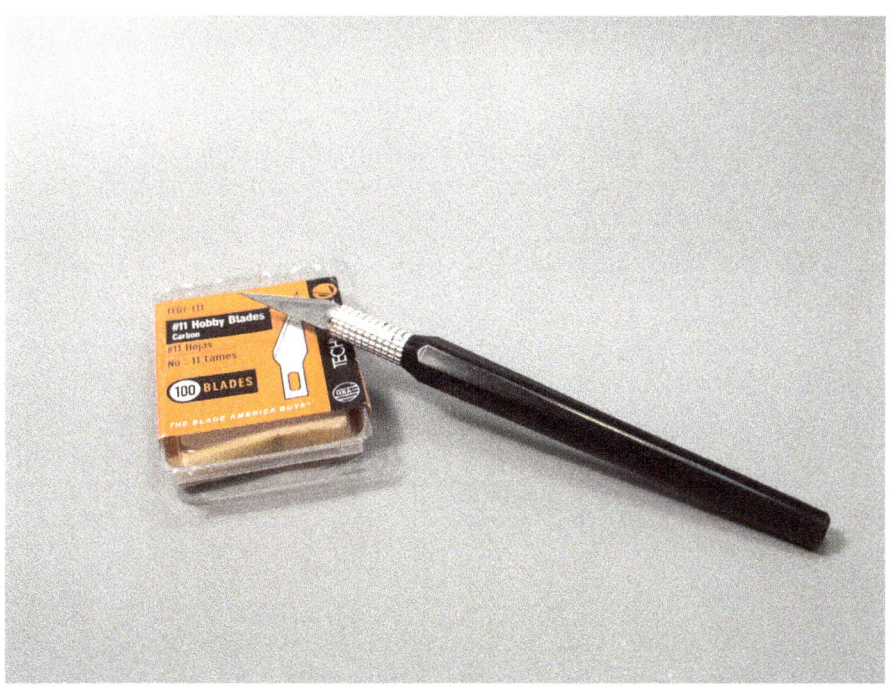

A hobby knife with a new sharp blade.

A pair of snips and textured pliers for a better grip.

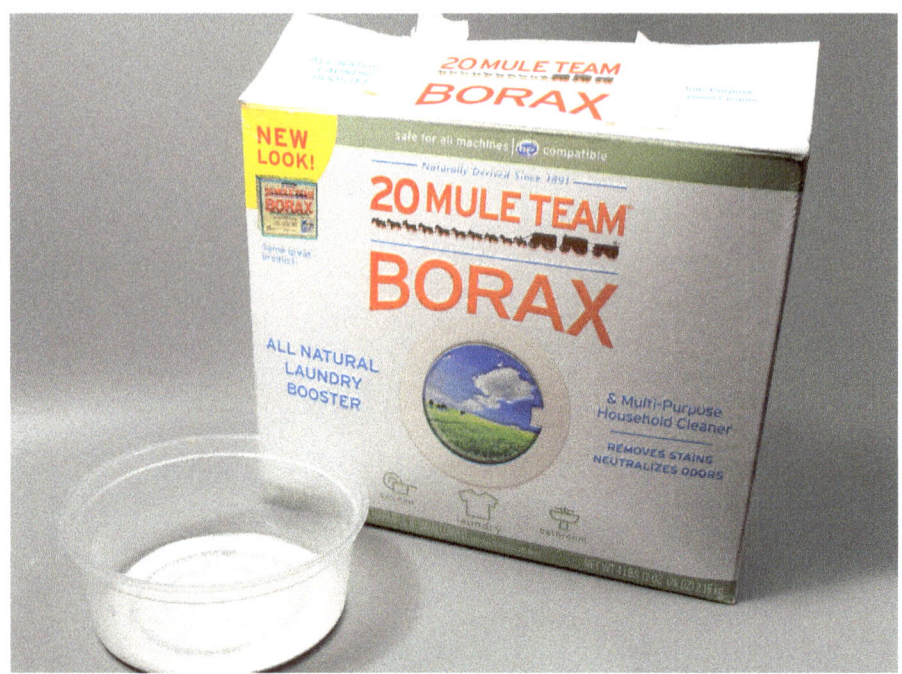

A small amount of borax, in a container that can accommodate the mouse pelt.

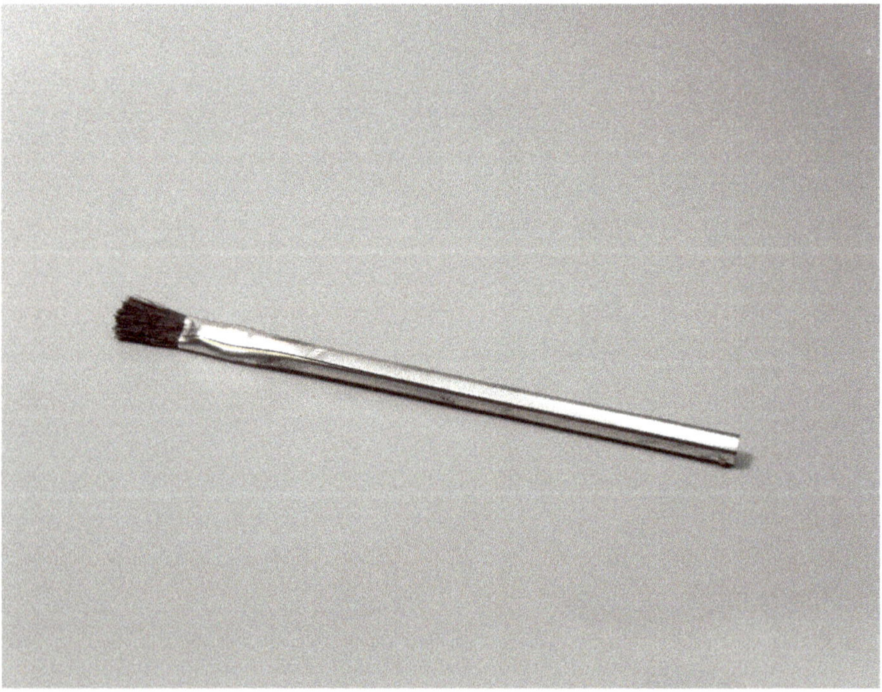

An acid brush, or soft toothbrush.

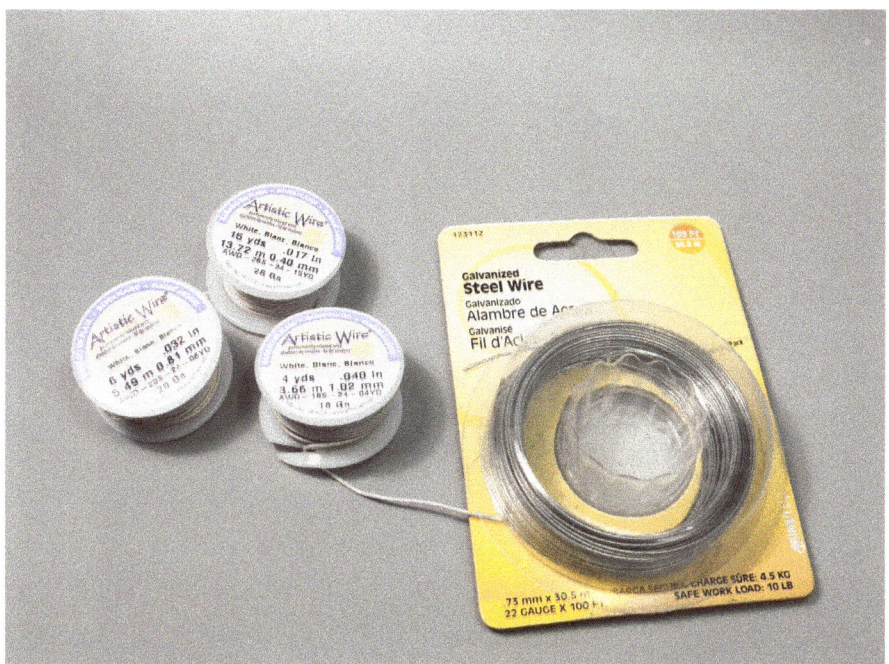

Metal wire (ideally gauge 20 for the legs, 24 for the arms and neck, even thinner for the tail).

A ¼ inch thick wooden square with two small holes for the feet, on which to mount your mouse..

A tiny bit of polyester fill for the tail and legs.

Skinning

The first thing to do is pull the mouse out of the freezer. Depending on the ambient temperature, it will take one to two hours to thaw. Leave it to thaw naturally, or if the ambient temperature is really low, put the frozen mouse under the gentle heat of a desk lamp.

Before you start, you might want to put on latex or nitrile gloves and a surgical mask.

I don't wear gloves, as I like to feel what I'm doing, but I do wear a surgical/dust mask to make sure I don't touch my face while I'm working.

On my video a lot of irate viewers leave rude comments scolding me for not wearing gloves. The simple reason for my not wearing gloves is that I'm not performing surgery on a live mouse, thus there's no need to prevent any post-surgical infections. Also, I use feeder mice that were bred in a lab, not road kill or wild animals. They're clean, disease-free and they don't smell bad.

It's all a matter of personal preference, but if you want to be on the safe side, wear gloves.

First of all, feel the mouse and make sure it's thawed. You should be able to bend the spine and spread out the limbs. If it's still a little stiff around the belly, that's fine, you can start on it and the heat from your hands will do the rest as you work.

If you're planning on standing the mouse on its hind legs like a human, in an anthropomorphic pose, make the incision in the back. If you want to mount it on all fours, like a real mouse, make the initial cut on the belly so the stitching will be hidden.

This tutorial will be describing how to make an anthropomorphic mouse, since that is what I'm most familiar with.

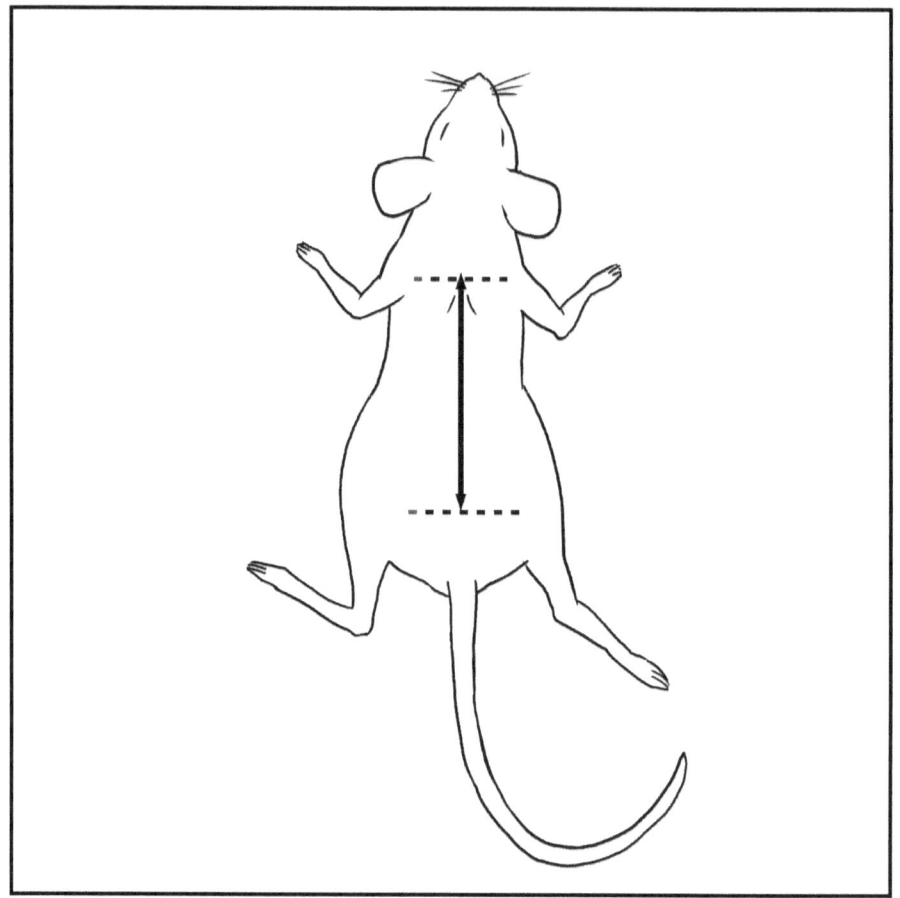

To start, trace the spine of the mouse with your finger. You're going to make a 1 inch vertical incision along the spine with your X-Acto knife. It's very important that you start with a new blade, because you want a clean cut. I can tell right away when it's not a new blade.

Start a little below the neck, apply enough pressure to cut the skin, but not so much that you slice through to the muscle. Stop the incision a little above the tail. You only want the incision to be big enough to pull the body through. But if it's too small, it might tear, so don't be over-optimistic.

The mouse should not bleed at any point during the process. If it bleeds, it's because you've cut too deep.

Using your fingers and the blade, start pulling the skin away from the body. When you use the knife, make sure you only cut the connective tissue by orienting the blade toward the body, so you don't cut the skin accidentally. You want to keep the skin intact, free of holes or cuts. While you can fix some small booboos with super glue, it's just simpler to avoid mistakes at the beginning. Go slowly, until you feel more confident.

Peel off the thigh and push on the leg from the outside to expose the joint. Use your blade to locate the joint and lift it up. Grab your snips and cut the joint.

Do the same on the other side, so the legs are no longer connected to the body, only by the skin.

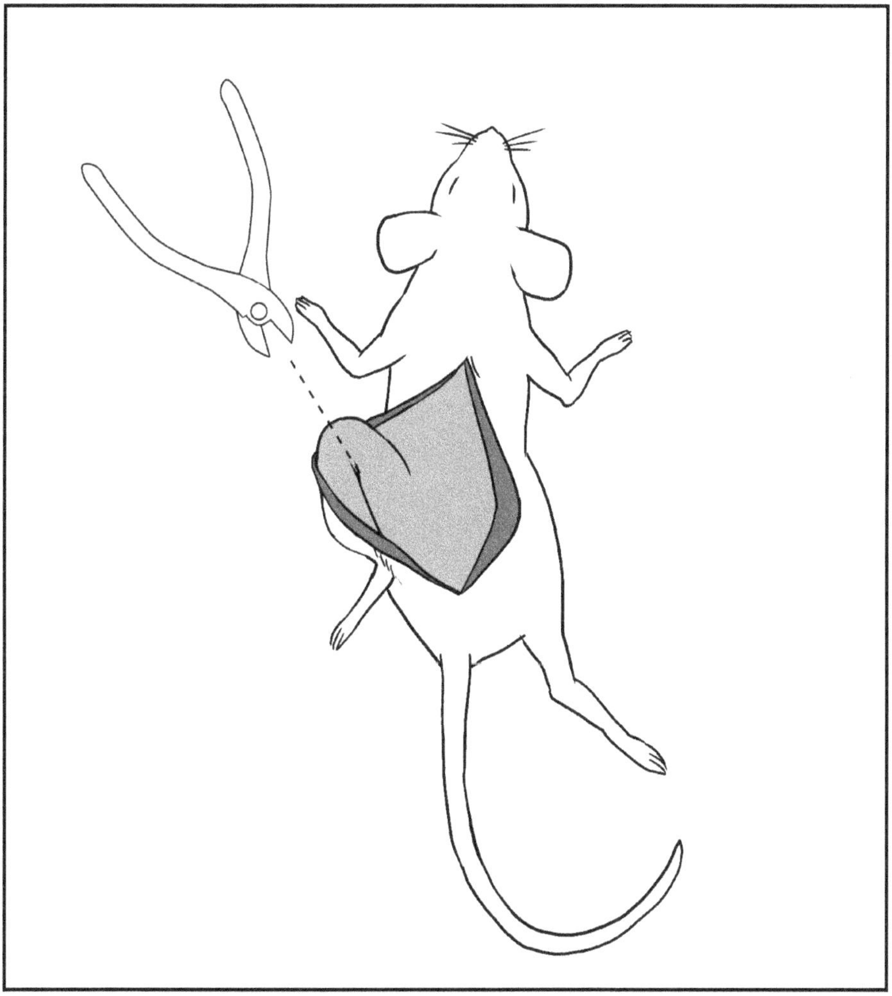

Next we move up and do the same for the shoulders. Push the arm up and expose the elbow. Lift the joint with the knife, and cut at the joint with the snips.

Now we want to separate the skin around the belly. Start by flipping the skin inside out, so you can peel it off the body more easily. Use your knife carefully: the abdominal membrane that contains the organs and intestines is very thin, and if you cut into it, you might get some gut spillage and it makes it more difficult to work. We are not eviscerating, we are skinning.

Cut the connective tissue around the belly until you reach the other side and you get a skin hammock. Separate the skin down to the tail, then focus back up on the head.

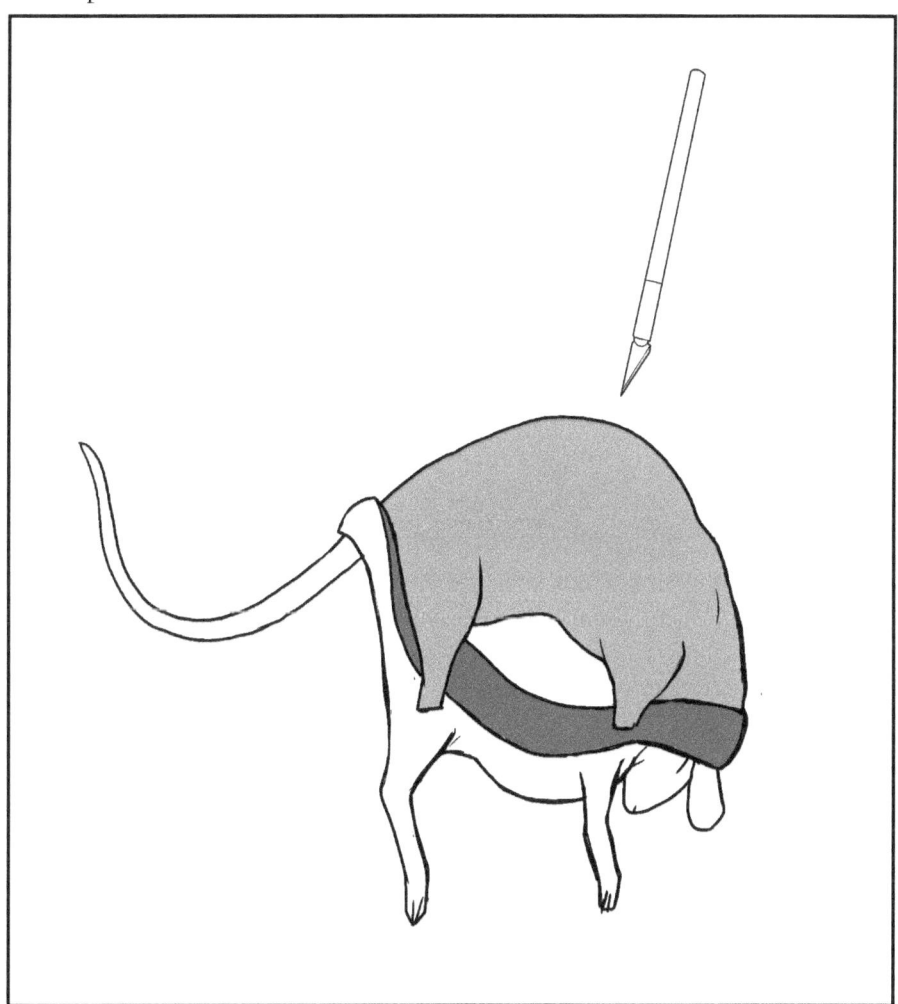

The skin should be flipped up over the mouse's head now. Keeping the skin tight with the fingers of your other hand, use the knife to cut through the ear canals, and then move along the skull and jaw. Locate the eyes. At this point, a fresh blade makes it easier to cut through the eyelids without any damage. Use small cuts along the orbit of the eye, staying close to the bone, to separate the eye lids. Leave the eyeballs behind with the body. You should end up with two neat little holes for the eyes.

Keep working toward the tip of the nose. Be careful around the mouth and lips. The bottom jaw shouldn't be too hard, and then you'll only be connected by the tip of the nose. I like to keep the upper teeth on the mouse.

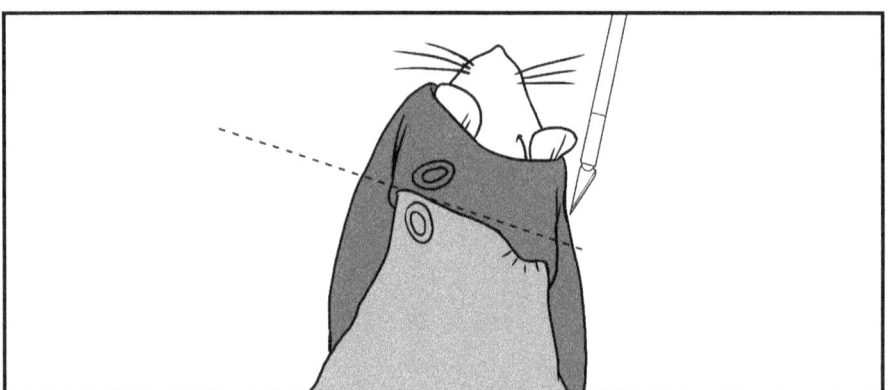

Grab your snips and orient them at an angle so you'll cut the bone at the tip of the muzzle, but include the teeth with your skin. The snips might slip along the bone as you squeeze, so be firm and quick.

Now that the head is free, move to the rear to deglove the tail. Using your knife, cut the connective tissue all the way around and down to the tail, exposing about 5mm, or a ¼ inch of the tail. Take the pliers (preferably textured ones so it doesn't slide), and use them to grab hold of the exposed part of the tail.

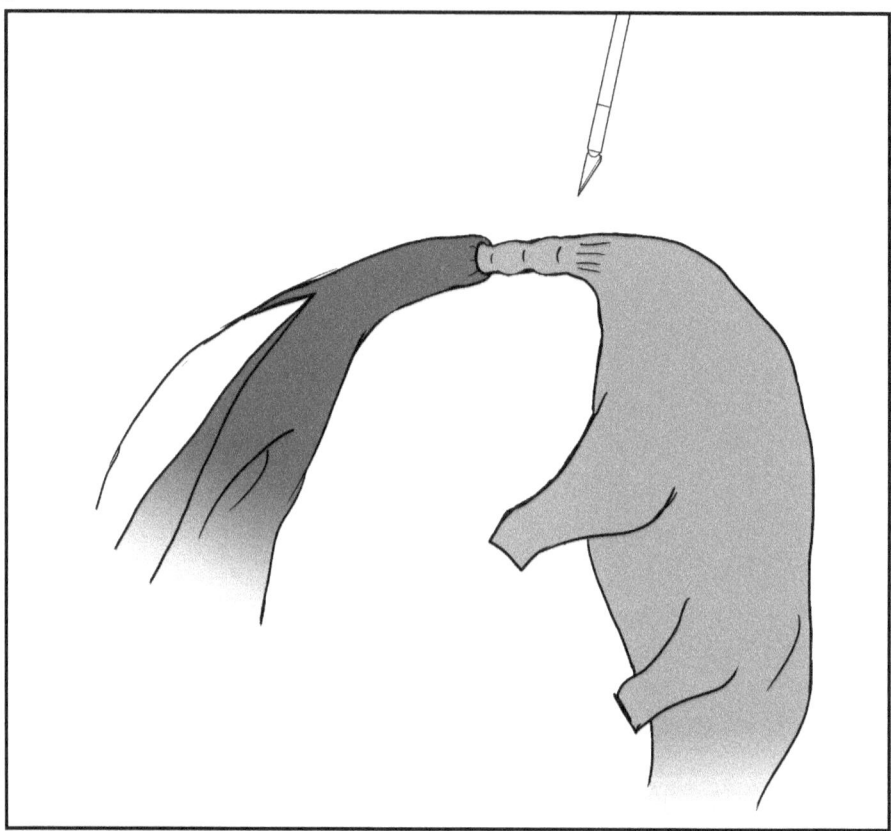

Using your thumbnail, slowly pull the skin off the tail bone. Go around the circumference if it's stubborn, exposing more and more as you go. At some point, it will give and it should slide out cleanly, like a glove, without flipping the tail skin inside out.

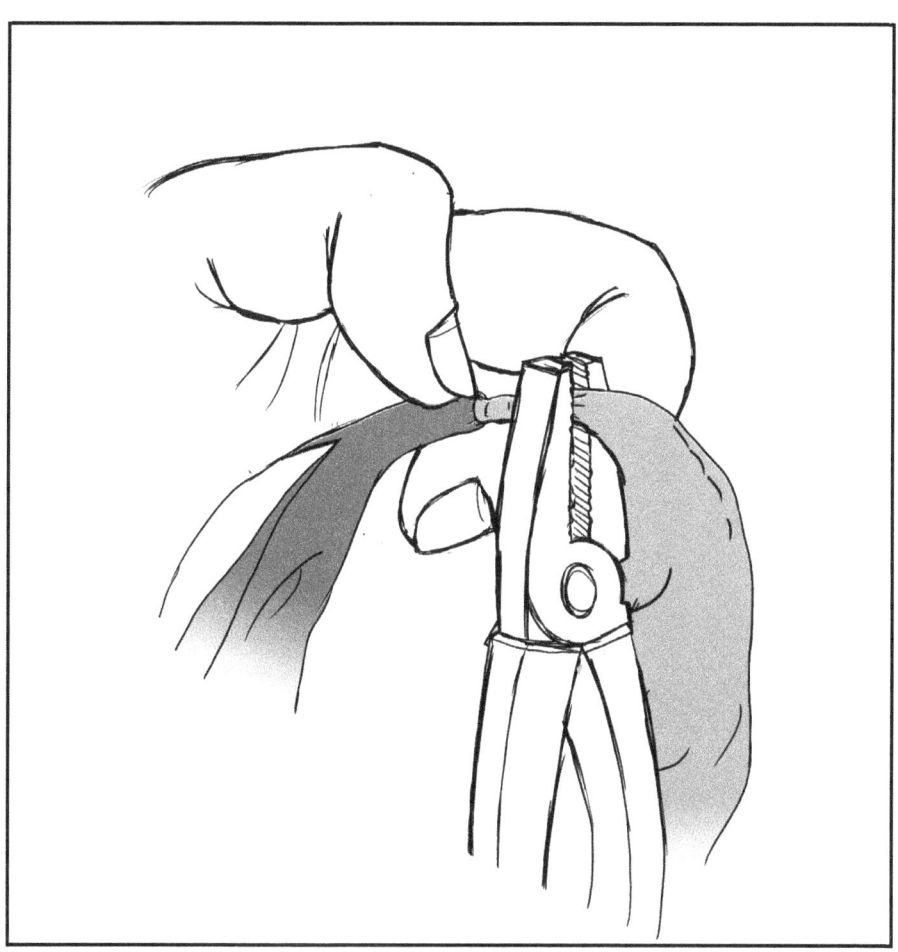

You now have two parts: the skin and the body. If this is your first time, lay the body in front of you for reference, to sculpt the head and body.

First, let's go wash the skin in the utility sink. Hold the skin under clean, gently running water, turn it inside out to wash the inside, then back out to wash the fur. I don't use any cleaning products. I've tried soap, shampoo, dishwashing soap and conditioner, but it removes too much oil in the mouse fur, making it more difficult to fluff it back up as it dries.

Gently squeeze the excess water and roll the pelt in a sheet of paper towel so it doesn't dry up while we make the body.

Stuffing

There are two parts to the body: the head and the body proper. I use different materials for each. I sculpt the head out of polymer clay (Sculpey or Fimo), so I get enough details in the face, and I file down polyurethane foam to shape the body.

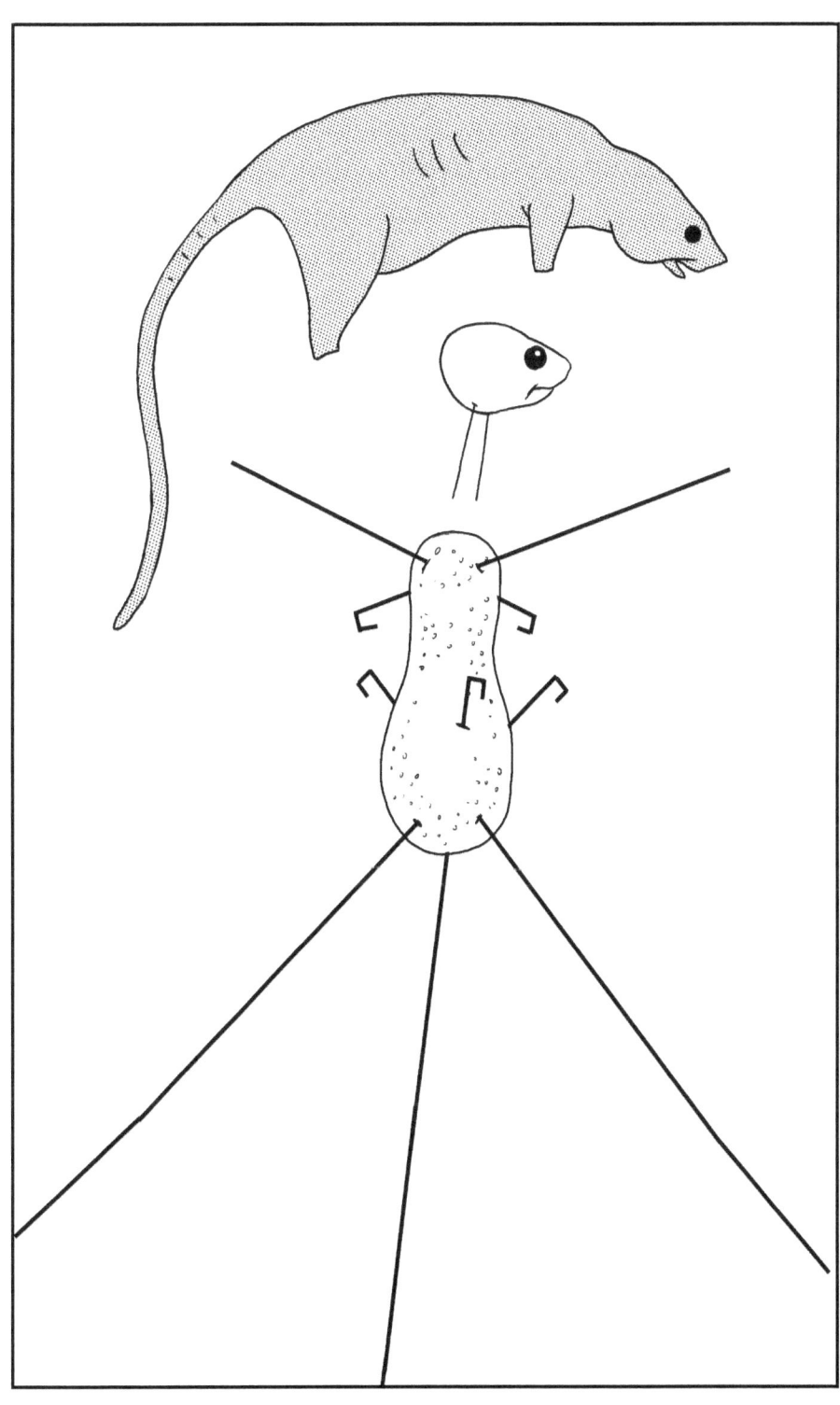

First let's make the head. Reference the real head for shape and size. Roll a lump of skin-colored polymer clay into a ball and, using whatever tools your have available, sculpt it to resemble the real head as closely as possible. At first you may tend to make it bigger than it really is, so make sure you make frequent side-by-side comparisons. If it's too big, the skin will be stretched too tight and the eyes might move out of alignment as it dries, and leave a gap.

I use 4mm black beads for the eyes. You can, if you wish, go a little smaller for more realism. First, hold the clay head next to the real head and mark the spot where the eyes should go. If your bead has holes, orient it so the holes are on top and bottom, not in front where it will show. Press the beads halfway into the clay. They should protrude out enough so that they will show through the eyelids. If needed, fill the bead holes with polymer clay, to secure the bead into place.

Cut two pieces of wire about 1 ½ inches long (or 3.5cm) for the neck. Using pliers, bend a U at the very tip and squish it down to create a little nub, then push the wires into the head from underneath, nubs first, where it will connect to the body. Press a little bit of clay around the wires, and the nubs will make sure the wires won't pull out once it's baked.

Place the sculpted head on a cookie sheet and bake, following directions for the polymer clay you're using.

While the head is baking, let's make the body. Using a serrated knife or a small saw, cut a piece of white polyurethane foam into a brick a little bigger than the size of the mouse's body. With a rasp or file, trim it and shape it so it matches the real body.

Cut two wires for the arms, two for the legs and one for the tail. Matching the limbs of the body, insert the wires so it mimics the limbs of the mouse, as well as the tail. On the back side, use pliers to bend a square hook at the end. Do not push the hooks into the body yet!

By now the head should be done baking. Remove it from the oven and let it cool for five minutes so it hardens properly.

Pour enough borax powder to cover the bottom of a clean, shallow deli container. Turn the skin inside out, and pat the flesh side dry with the paper towel. Pull off any pieces of fat or flesh that remain on it. Be very careful not to tear the skin.

Now dredge the skin into the borax and make sure to get some powder everywhere onto the flesh side of the skin. Shake off the excess.

Let's stuff the tail.

We need a piece of wire that can reach to the end of it. Cut a wire to about 6 inches, or 15cm long.

Using the wire, stuff a small amount of borax all the way into the tail.

Now bend a tiny hook, as small as possible, at the end of the wire. Take a piece of polyester fluff and elongate it a little.

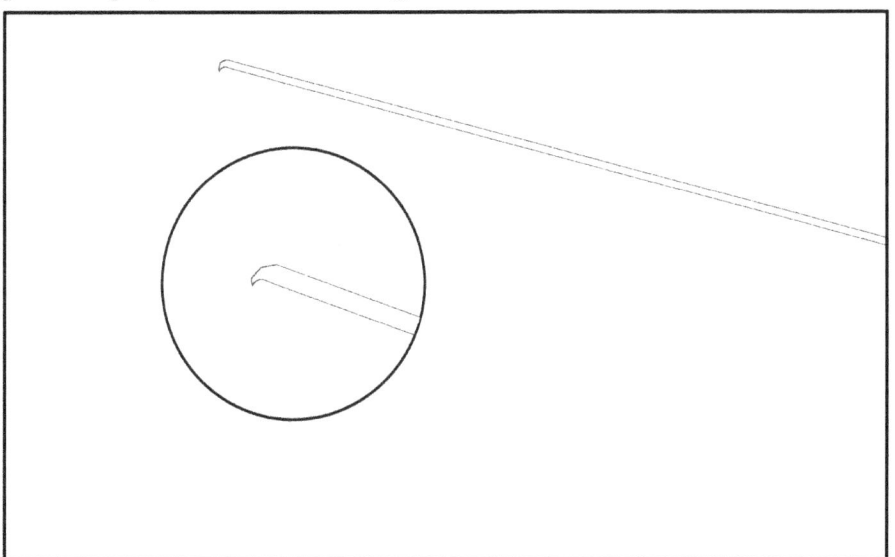

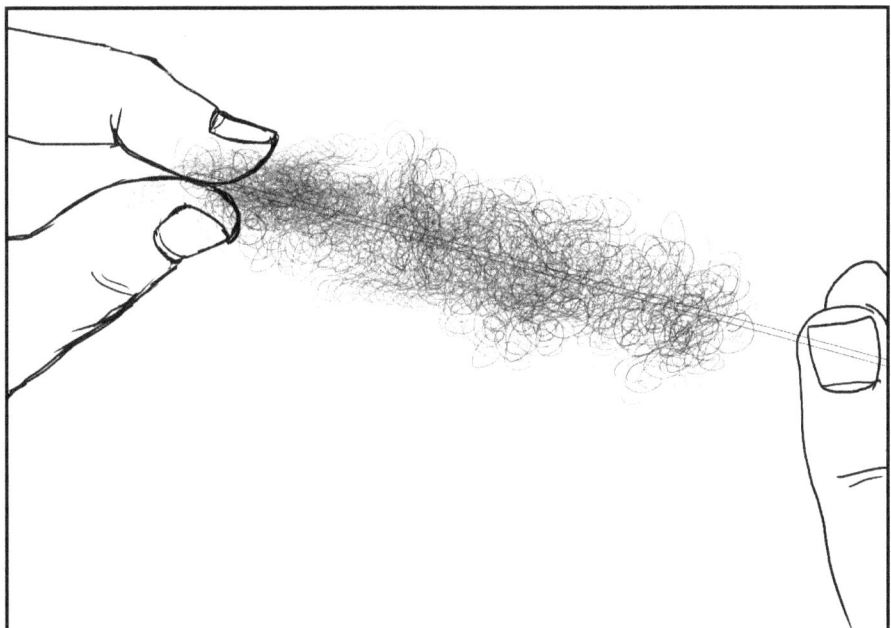

Hold it over the hook, and turn the wire slowly so the small hook will catch the fluff. Once it catches, keep turning the wire and make a tiny sausage that's the girth and length of the tail. Insert it into the tail, pushing and turning carefully as far down as possible. I can't ever reach the very end, so don't worry too much about it.

Wiggle the wire out, turning it around until it unhooks from the fluff and you can slip it out, leaving the fluff behind in the tail.

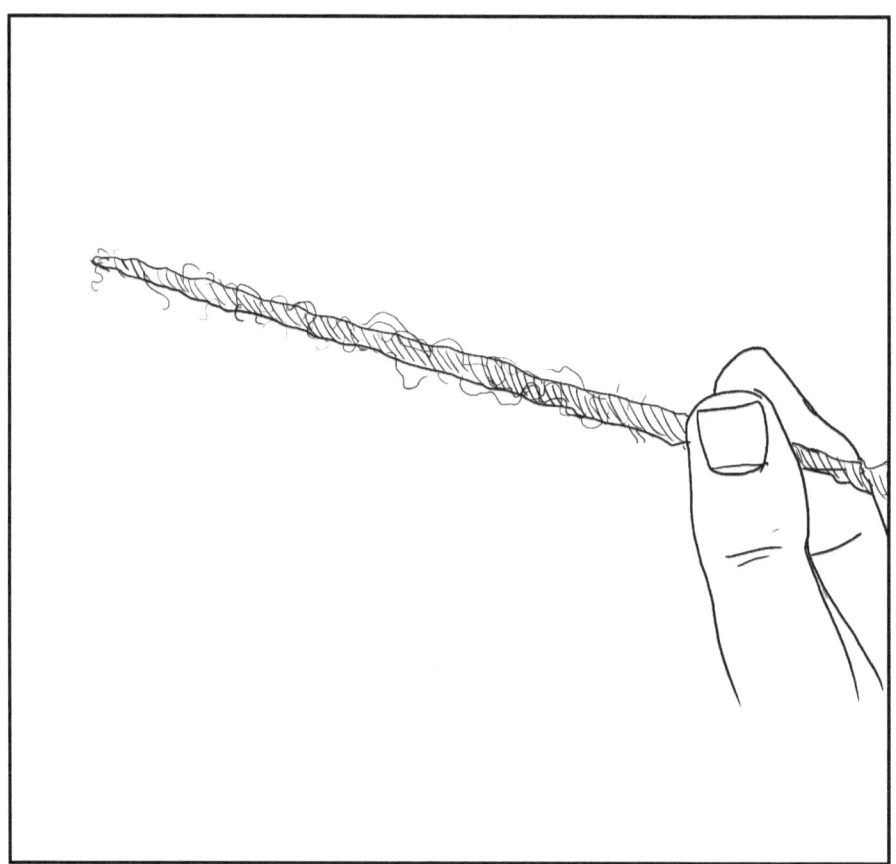

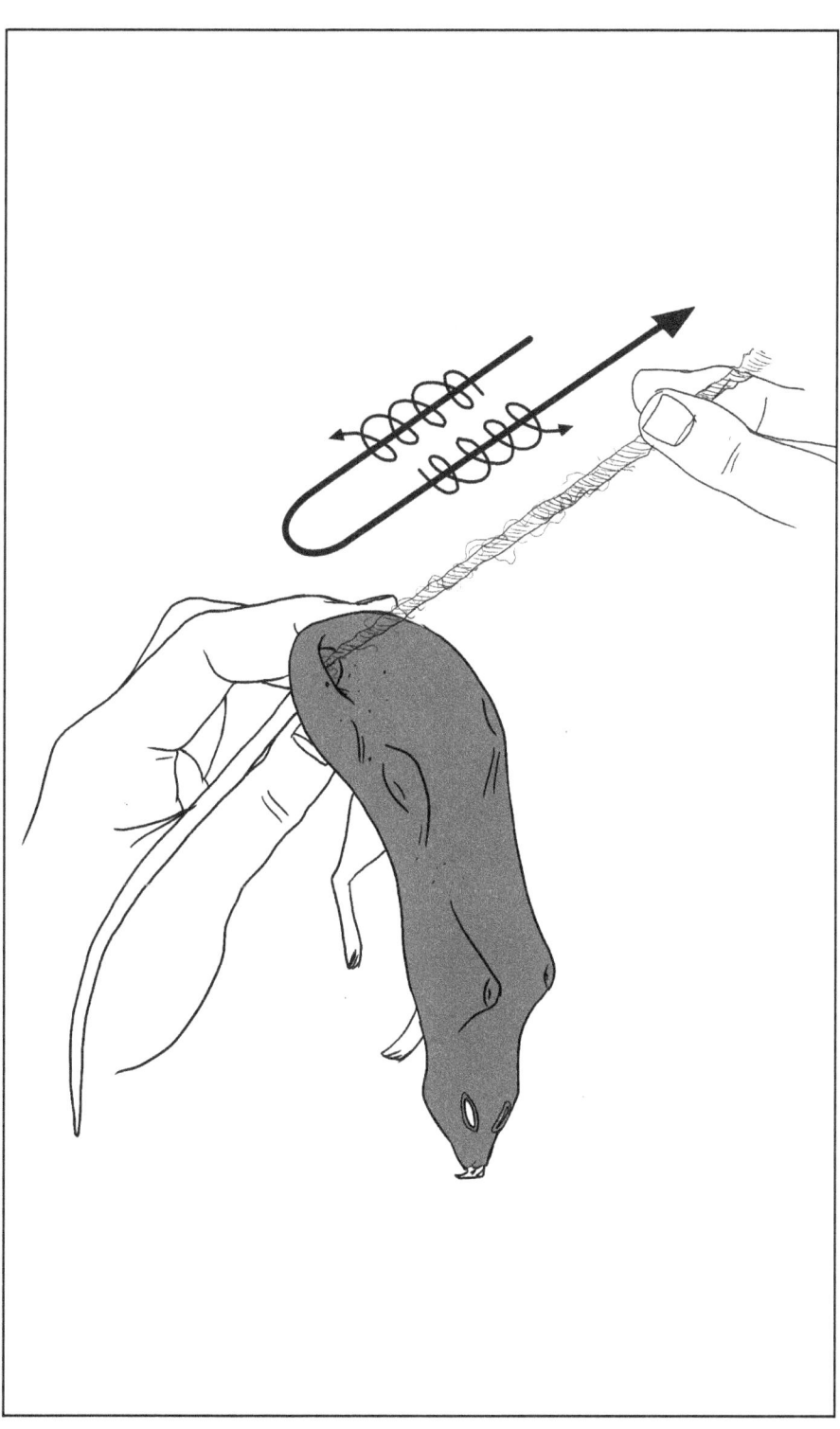

The mouse's skin should still be inside out at this point. Take the head shape and cut both wires to the same length, at an angle so they end in a sharp point, about ½ inch long, or 1.3cm. Now place the tip of the nose against the tip of the nose on the skin, making sure that it is oriented correctly, and flip the skin over it so the shape finds itself inside the skin, eyes showing through the eyelids.

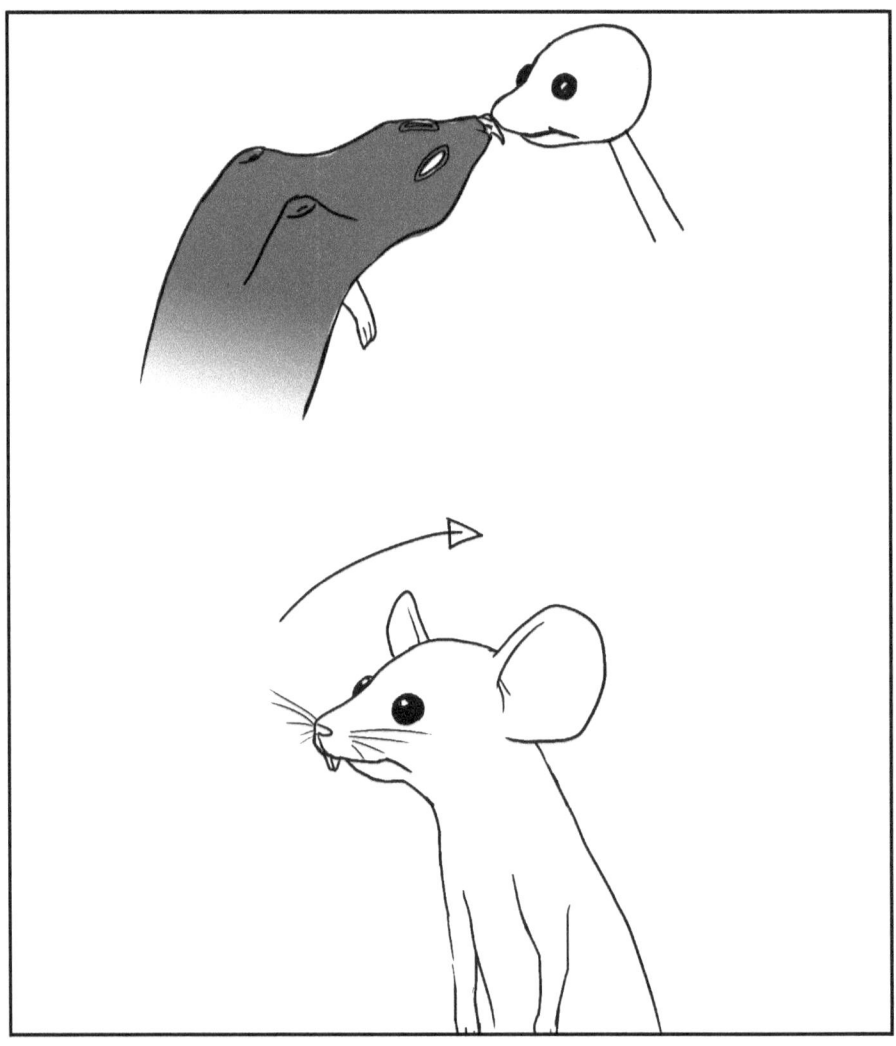

Continue and flip the whole skin so the fur is on the outside.

On the foam body, cut the front ends of the arm wires into a sharp point, and pull them back towards the hooks so the sharp ends are flush with the foam.

Pull the tail wire all the way through and push the hooked end into the foam to secure it.

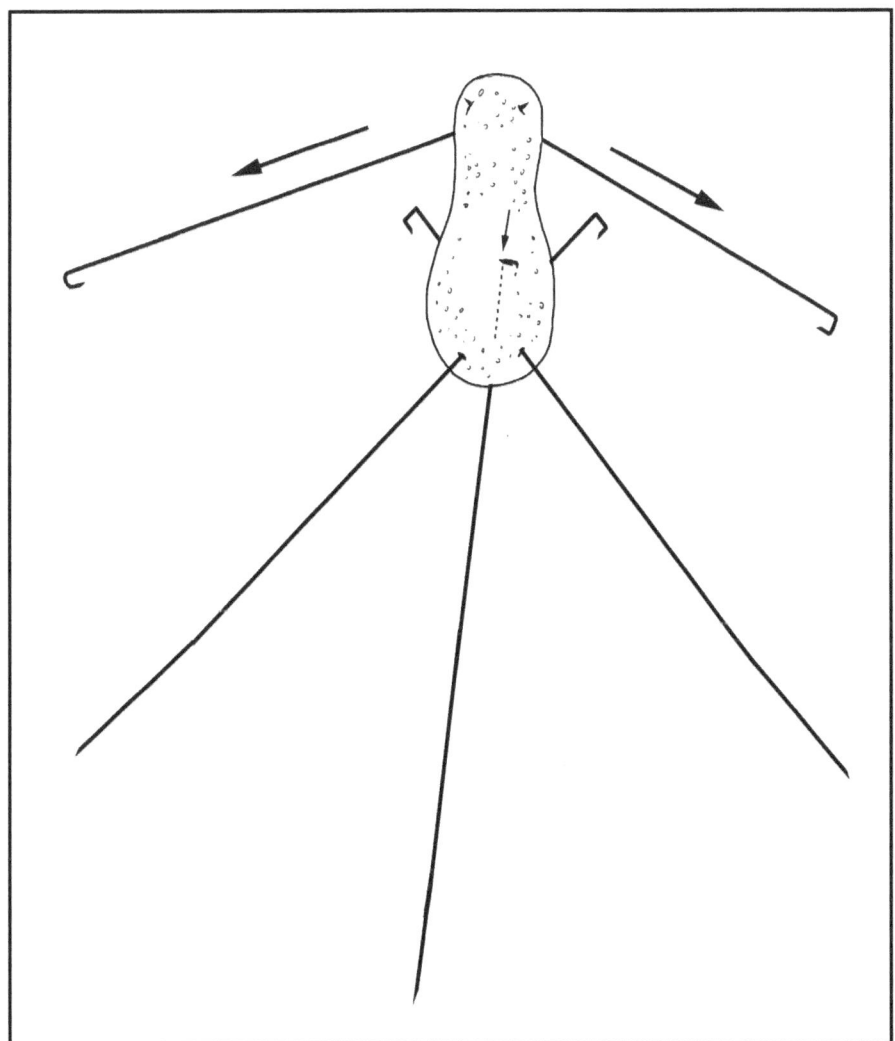

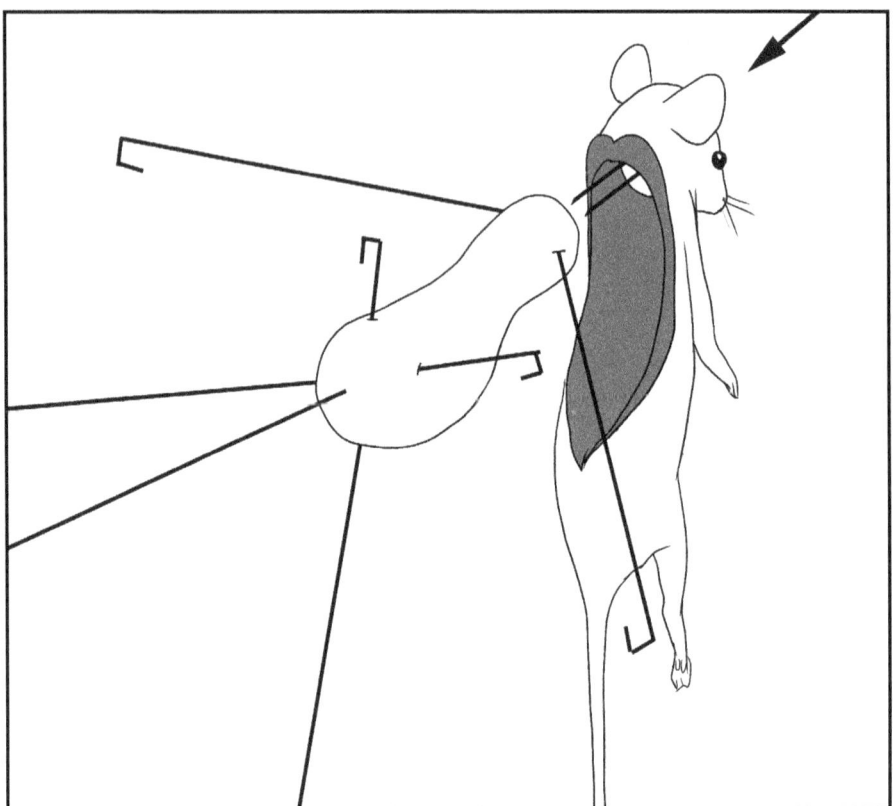

Line up the neck wires and press the head into the foam body. Be careful not to pinch the skin between the two parts before connecting them.

One at a time, slowly push the arm wire into the arm of the mouse, along the bone, past the "elbow", which is really the heel, and into the pad. Poke though the skin and out in the middle of the "palm" all the way, and push the hook into the foam at the back to secure and hide it. Repeat on the other side.

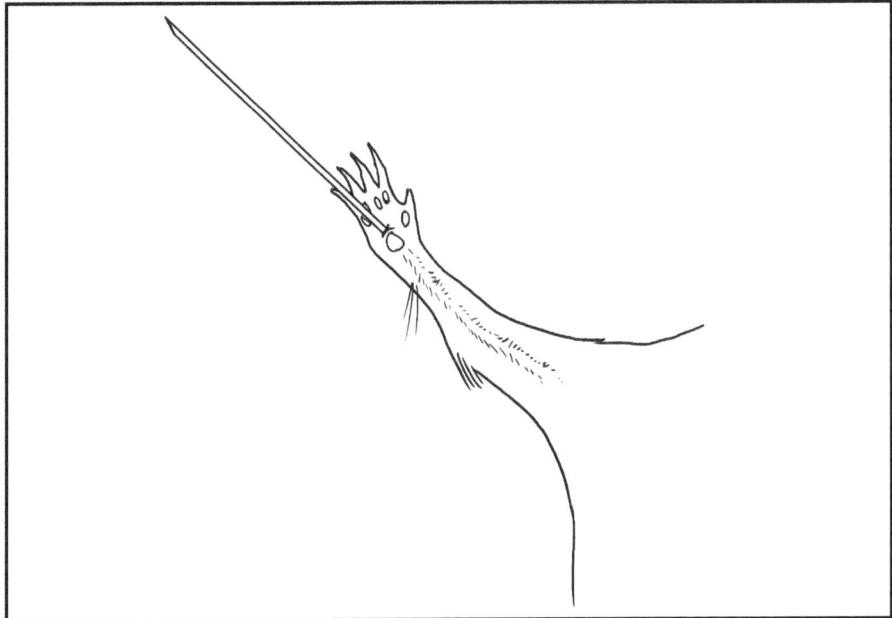

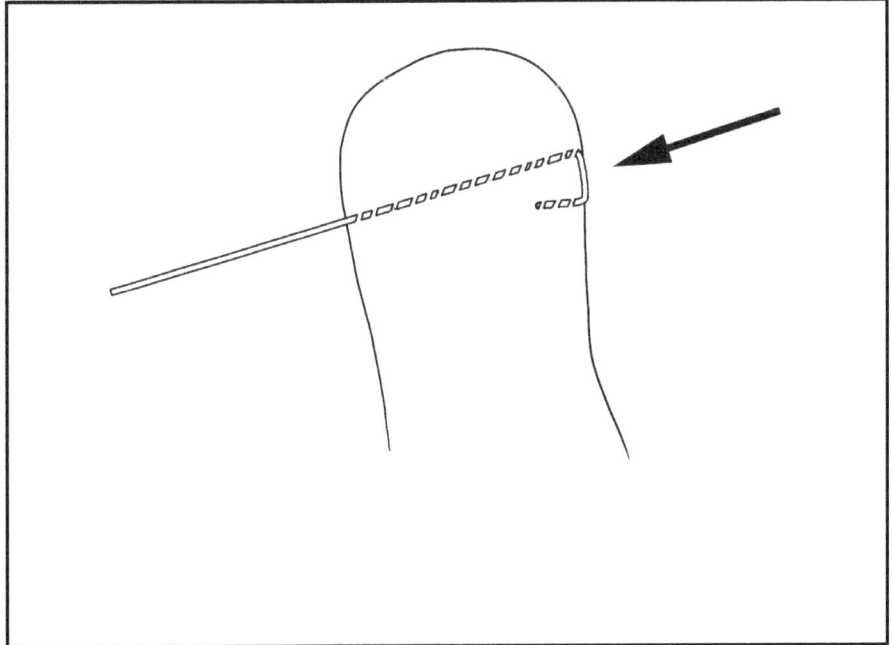

Cut the tail and leg wires into a sharp point, and pull the leg wires out so the front end is flush with the body.

Thread the tail wire into the tail, careful not to poke through the skin before the end. Push it through the end of the tail, and pull it all the way, while helping the skin fit over the rear of the body.

Now the whole body should be inside the skin.

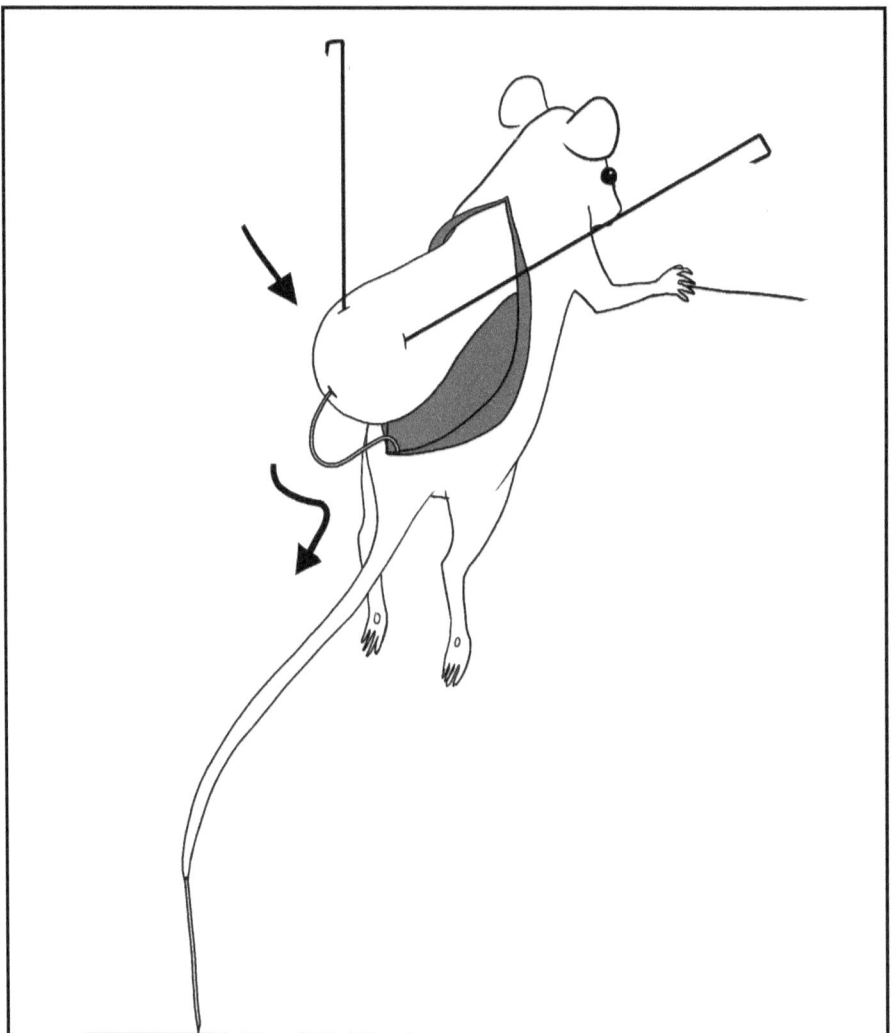

Just like the arms, push each leg wire along the leg bone of the mouse, pierce the skin under the pad and pull the wires all the way through. Push the hooks into the foam to secure and hide the wires.

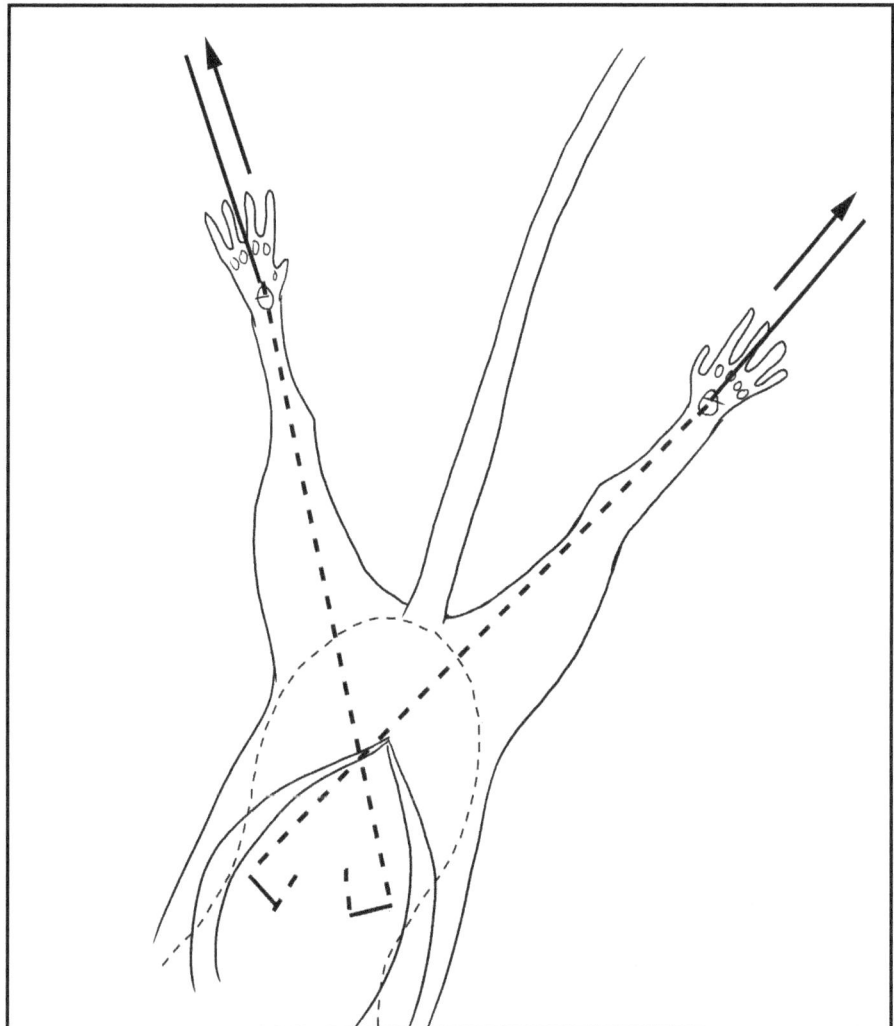

You can now adjust the shape by stuffing small amounts of polyester fluff into the thighs, belly or shoulders, depending on the silhouette you're trying to achieve. If you stuff the limbs, make sure you use an equal amount of fluff on both sides so it remains symmetrical.

To sew the mouse up, thread a small needle with some cotton or polyester thread. Pick the thread to match the color of your mouse. Make a knot at the end.

It doesn't matter whether you start at the top or bottom of the incision.

Start on the flesh side, at the very end of the incision, and continue in a baseball stitch along the seam.

Secure with a surgeon's knot.

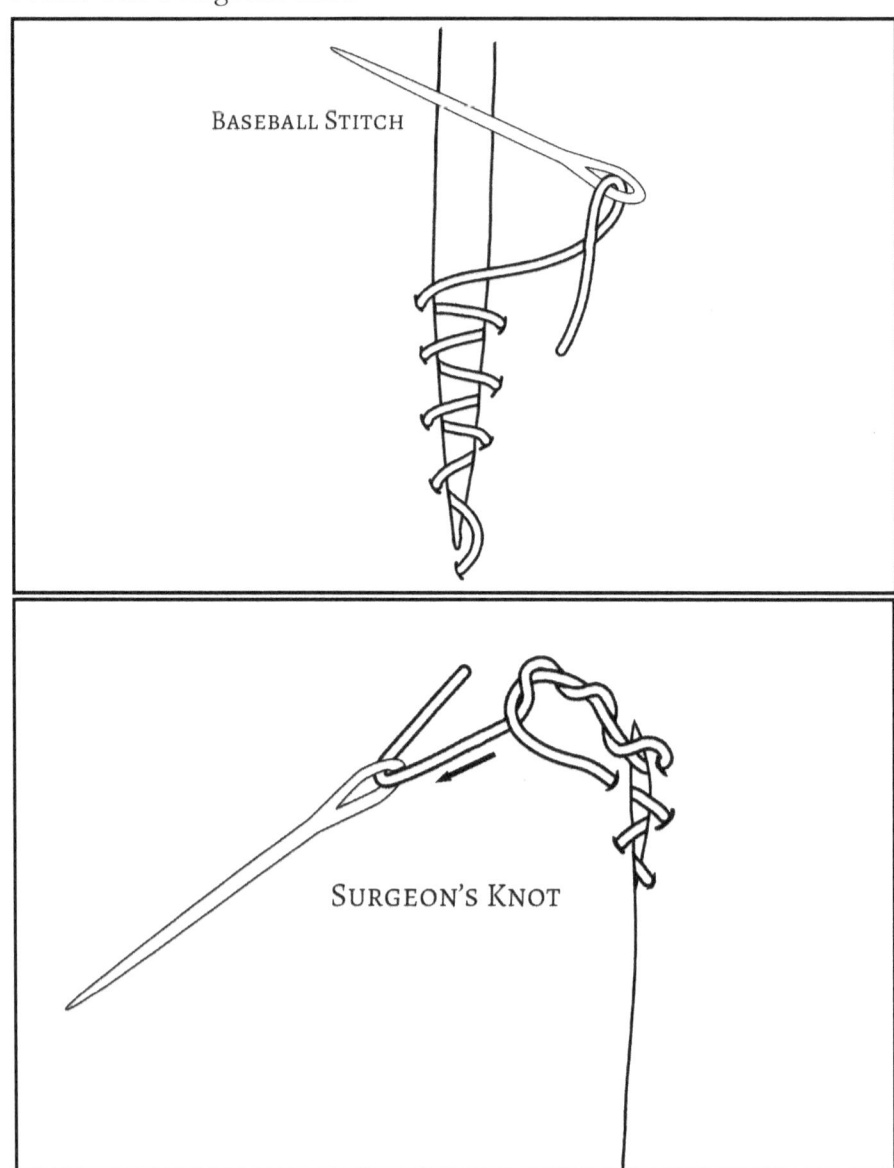

Posing

Now is the time to decide how to pose your mouse. Professionals call it "mounting". On a small wooden square, drill two holes where the foot wires will go. The spacing will determine the mouse's stance. The holes should be just big enough for the wire to go through.

Push the feet wires through and under the pedestal. Make sure the legs are long enough when the toes rest on the "ground". Bend the wires under the pedestal to secure them. If this is a temporary mount, leave the length of wire and bend it up over the top of the wood until it dries.

For a permanent mount, you can bend the wires and push them into the wood underneath, and then cover them with felt or another piece of wood to hide them.

Use the wires to gently bend the arms, legs and tail to achieve the pose you want. You have to make your decision now, because once the mouse is dry, you won't be able to move it anymore. Make sure you're happy with it.

Outfits

If you've gone this far and are holding a mounted mouse in your hand, with or without clothes, you should be proud of yourself. Well done!

I am mentioning the outfits at the end, but as I said earlier, you should have made the outfits before making the mouse. Hopefully you were paying attention, otherwise: "Surprise!"

Immediately after you mount the mouse on the pedestal, while it's soft, put the clothes and accessories on, glue and sew them in place, tighten the belts, strap on the bags and backpacks, and pose the mouse so everything looks good from every possible angle. Then you can put it aside to dry, and don't touch it for a week or so.

Costumes can be as simple or elaborate as you choose, it's your mouse!

Conclusion

In conclusion, there is no conclusion. I'm still doing mice, although I took a big break this summer to write this.

I'm surprised I'm not bored with them yet, but I'm thinking about moving on to more dynamic poses. I might even break some of my rules. There are infinite possibilities to explore!

We shall find out what Patricia and I come up with in the future. We already have a couple of ideas brewing, but as we learned, nothing really ever goes according to plan. It's good to leave the door open to the unexpected, and just follow your muse. I'll follow mine and you find yours.

And as Dickens' Mr. Micawber kept saying in David Copperfield: "Something will turn up."

As for you, go out and get inspired, or stay in and make something. Be creative! It will make you feel good.

You're welcome.

Thank you for reading, I hope you enjoyed it.

You can follow my mice on Facebook, Instagram, Twitter, Tumbler, Pinterest and Etsy, under the name LeHeartDesign.

I will see you around on the internet, or at a convention.

Au revoir, et merci.

Mai

Pirate Black Bart

Although you can't see it in this picture, my pirates wear their eyepatch around their neck, like most pirates used to. Why, you ask?

When a pirate ship intercepted another ship, the pirates used to swarm aboard and take over. The pirates would make their way below decks, or downstairs as we landlubbers would say, to where the crew of the boarded ship had retreated. The poor fellows would wait for their attackers, under the safety of darkness, to come below from the bright sunshine outside, hoping to ambush the pirates and hack them to pieces before their vision could adjust to the low light conditions.

Knowing this, any pirate worth his salt would cover one eye with a patch before the boarding, to then flip it up when he had to run below deck, so that he would not be rendered completely blind by the sudden descent from brilliant sunshine into gloom.

This way, one eye would already be accustomed to darkness.

Clever pirates!

Conclusion

Tiny Dancers

About the Authors

Léa Mai Nguyen is a French-born taxidermy artist who lives in Marin County, California with her wife and son. After abandoning a 20-year career in video games, she became a mouse taxidermist in 2014. She sells her life-like taxidermy mice in handmade costumes through curio stores like Paxton Gate in San Francisco and Portland, in person at events throughout the San Francisco Bay Area, as well as on Etsy.

Patricia Fitzsimmons is a retired civil servant born in London, now living in the Southwest of England. Her interests include literature, archeology and history.

Together, they are the formidable duo behind the creations of Le Heart Design, la Crème de la Crème of Mouse Taxidermy.

www.ingramcontent.com/pod-product-compliance
Lightning Source LLC
Chambersburg PA
CBHW061219070526
44584CB00029B/3898